Praise for *Religious Liberty in Crisis*

"Seasoned, wise, magisterial, and gracefully written—a comprehensive judge's tour of the religious-freedom horizon. After 400 years as America's 'first liberty,' freedom of religion and conscience is under unprecedented assault, and Ken Starr's overview is essential for all who would make their stand with a depth of understanding as well as courage."

Os Guinness, author of *Last Call for Liberty*

"What does the Constitution have to say about religion and religious liberty? How has the US Supreme Court interpreted what the Constitution says? Where has the court gotten it right? Where have the justices erred—and why? Ken Starr, drawing on his experience as a lawyer who has argued some of the most important religious-freedom cases, answers these questions in this marvelously lucid and readable book."

Robert P. George, McCormick
Professor of Jurisprudence, Princeton University

"For many years, the United States has led efforts to reverse what has become a full-blown global crisis in religious freedom, as invidious discrimination and violent persecution spread to almost every region of the world. Now comes a major new work by one of America's foremost authorities on religious freedom, Judge Ken Starr, to warn us that America is facing its own crisis. The nation where religious liberty was once considered 'the first freedom' is now experiencing growing hostility to religion among its culture-forming institutions and its political elites. With powerful arguments and winsome prose, Judge Starr explains why America cannot afford the loss of religious freedom. Read *Religious Liberty in Crisis*, and you'll understand why the stakes could not be higher—for America, or for the world—and how we all, religious or not, must be a part of the solution."

Thomas Farr, president, Religious Freedom Institute

"Judge Starr's book is elegantly written and an excellent summary of religious freedom in America. Covering all of the major cases, yet presenting them as the stories they are, he also includes his own personal involvement in some of the biggest cases in our nation's history, making this book a fascinating read that all will enjoy. It is both a celebration and a warning to all Americans who care about religious freedom."

Kelly Shackelford, Esq., president and CEO,
First Liberty Institute

"My friend, Ken Starr, decided to tackle the challenging topic of religious freedom. I encourage everyone to take this opportunity to learn from one of the greatest legal minds in our country and empower themselves with the facts to push back against the misinformation in our classrooms."

Charlie Kirk, founder and president,
Turning Point USA

"Ken Starr has been a friend of mine for years. I haven't just heard about what Ken believes to be true about his faith, I've seen it in the way he loves God, his beautiful family, and his neighbors, both near and far away. In this book, Ken takes us on a meaningful and heartfelt journey. He reminds us of where we have been as a country, and points toward a bright future which is available to us if we have the courage to pursue it. This book contains some hard truths, delivered by a profoundly kind and knowledgeable man."

Bob Goff, author of *New York Times* bestsellers
Love Does, Everybody, Always, and *Dream Big,*
and honorable consul for the
Republic of Uganda to the United States

"I knew this book would be informative. After all, Ken Starr is the author. He is one of the most reliable sources of policy truth in our country. I knew this book would be relevant. The question of religious liberty is increasingly up for grabs. What I didn't expect, and was pleased to discover, is that this book is a page turner! A person needn't be a law school graduate or policy nerd to get caught up in the conversation of these chapters. Second only to a dinner with Ken Starr himself, this book is the best opportunity for a fresh look at an essential topic."

Max Lucado, pastor and
New York Times bestselling author

RELIGIOUS

LIBERTY

IN CRISIS

RELIGIOUS LIBERTY IN CRISIS

Exercising Your Faith
in an Age *of* Uncertainty

KEN STARR

Encounter
BOOKS

New York • London

First American edition published in 2021 by Encounter Books,
an activity of Encounter for Culture and Education, Inc.,
a nonprofit, tax-exempt corporation.
Encounter Books website address: www.encounterbooks.com

Manufactured in the United States and printed on
acid-free paper. The paper used in this publication meets
the minimum requirements of ANSI/NISO Z39.48–1992
(R 1997) (*Permanence of Paper*).

FIRST AMERICAN EDITION

Published in association with Yates & Yates, www.yates2.com

LIBRARY OF CONGRESS CATALOGING-IN-PUBLICATION DATA

Names: Starr, Kenneth, 1946– author.
Title: Religious Liberty in Crisis: Exercising Your Faith
in an Age of Uncertainty / by Ken Starr.
Description: First American Edition. | New York: Encounter Books, 2021.
Includes bibliographical references and index. |
Identifiers: LCCN 2020041713 (print) | LCCN 2020041714 (ebook)
ISBN 9781641771801 (Hardcover: acid-free paper) | ISBN 9781641771818 (eBook)
Subjects: LCSH: Freedom of religion—United States. | Civil rights—United
States. Classification: LCC KF4783.S73 2021 (print) | LCC KF4783 (ebook)
DDC 342.7308/52—dc23
LC record available at https://lccn.loc.gov/2020041713
LC ebook record available at https://lccn.loc.gov/2020041714

Interior page design and typesetting by Bruce Leckie

Dedication

To several of my many heroes of religious liberty, beginning with the enduring memory of Sam Ericsson, who taught an entire generation of lawyers to be justice warriors; Tom Farr, diplomat, author, and founder of the Religious Freedom Institute; Bob Fu, survivor of the Tiananmen Square massacre and who teaches the entire world to care deeply about humanity's first freedom; Kevin "Seamus" Hasson, founder and long-serving President of the Becket Fund; Mark Martin, the distinguished chief justice (emeritus) of the North Carolina Supreme Court and now dean of the Regent Law School; Allan Sears, a bold pioneer in religious-freedom litigation, and to Mike Farris, a hero of the home-school movement who now leads Alliance Defending Freedom. Jay Sekulow, who was (and remains) powerfully effective at the Supreme Court podium; Kelly Shackelford, who founded and still leads the litigation and educational center, First Liberty Institute; and Frank Wolf, whose exemplary thirty-four-year career in Congress demonstrated the true meaning of selfless public service and dedication to the cause of religious freedom for all.

CONTENTS

INTRODUCTION

A PRELIMINARY WORD

Everyone has a story. So, too, does every country. The story of America is especially powerful and inspiring, and that power and inspiration is baked into our DNA.

What do I mean?

Our national DNA contains a dominant freedom gene. Why did men and women from other countries—the English, Dutch, French, and Spanish—choose to uproot themselves and find their way to a new home in an unknown land in the latter part of the eighteenth century? The answer for so many boiled down to one thing: the opportunity to enjoy freedom, including religious freedom.

Of course, many came involuntarily, trafficked under the inhumane yoke of slavery. They, too, shared the dream of freedom, longing for the day when the unjust practice would be abolished and they could participate fully in the American experience.

Years after the practice of slavery was cast off, Dr. Martin Luther King Jr.'s immortal "I have a dream" speech captured the longing of African-Americans for full participation in American liberty, crying out:

> [W]hen we allow freedom to ring, when we let it ring from every village and every hamlet, from every state and every city, we will be able to speed up that day when *all* of God's children, black men and white men, Jews and Gentiles, Protestants and Catholics, will be able to join hands and sing in the words of the old Negro spiritual, "Free at last! Free at last! Thank God Almighty, we are free at last!"

Dr. King chose his venue for this speech wisely. Silently gazing out on the civil rights leader and the hundreds of thousands of pro-freedom marchers, America's icon of freedom, Abraham Lincoln, sat on his chair flanked on either side by his words chiseled on the walls of his memorial. To the left were the immortal words of his Gettysburg Address: "Four score and seven years ago our fathers brought forth on this continent a new nation, conceived in liberty and dedicated to the proposition that all men are created equal."

Lincoln's words were true. A nation born in liberty and freedom was torn asunder by its original sin, the scourge of slavery. America needed to be cleansed and born again. Thus, the Gettysburg Address concluded with the call for the country's second birth, "that this nation, under God, shall have a new birth of freedom—and that government of the people, by the people, for the people, shall not perish from the earth."

As both Lincoln's inspiring address at Gettysburg and Dr. King's mighty speech at the base of the memorial demonstrate, at the heart of America's story is the fundamental human desire to be free. It's why we sing of the "sweet land of liberty." It's why, for the country's entire history, people have immigrated to America and precious few have emigrated from America.

Humans want freedom. Were it not for freedom, the land would be bitter, as it was in the Egypt of old when the displaced children of Israel suffered interminably under slavery's cruel yoke for more than 400 years. Were it not for freedom, people would be voting with their feet and moving to other countries, to some twenty-first century version of our own "sweet land of liberty." Were it not for freedom, thousands from across the globe—from Venezuela, Syria, or Cuba—wouldn't be leaving their homelands for a shot at entering America.

FREEDOM TO DO ONE THING
IS NOT FREEDOM TO DO ALL THINGS

Years ago, I popped into a waiting town car outside our law firm's offices in New York City's Citigroup building. Unless I'm obliged to be on my phone, invariably I ask drivers about their own story and on this particular day, as we headed across the East River toward LaGuardia Airport, the driver told me his. He had recently come to America from Albania. "Why?" I inquired, politely. His response embodied the human longing for liberty. "Very simple. In Albania, you can eat bread. You can eat bread anywhere. But in America you can eat bread in freedom."

My new friend from Albania was onto something. But freedom is not self-defining. It might be tempting to believe that since he was free to do one thing (eat bread wherever and whenever he pleased), he might do anything he wanted. But we all know that can't be right. After all, life within a community carries with it the inevitable restraints of law. I can't drive my car as fast as I want, even if no one else is on the road. If I'm traveling on foot, I can't take a short cut across someone's property if there's a fence with a "No trespassing" sign prominently displayed. In countless everyday ways, our freedom is rightly constrained.

The formal limitation on freedom is called law—or limitations enforceable by law. Justice Oliver Wendell Holmes, Jr., made the point well. As a basic constitutional right, Americans enjoy freedom of speech, but that freedom does not encompass shouting "Fire!" in a crowded theater. Liberty within a community necessarily has limits, based upon the felt needs of the social order.

Even in the current age of turmoil and division, Americans are truly blessed to live in a land of liberty. But our system is emphatically not libertarian in nature. In the age of COVID-19 (the context in which I'm writing this book), some communities require masks to participate in public commerce. In the age of increased Black Lives Matter demonstrations (also the context in which I'm writing this book), some communities require protesters to obtain permits or risk arrest for failure to comply with city ordinances. If anything is clear, it's that America is a country of "ordered liberty."[1]

Just as there are natural laws such as the one that, for example, limited my own athletic prowess (I was encouraged by a football coach to give up my gridiron dreams in the ninth grade—the curse of being too slow and scrawny), so, too, are there conventional laws, fashioned in our national, state, and local communities, that guide and direct our everyday life. If those laws are justly made, through a fair process in a representative democracy, I am obliged as a member of the community to abide by those laws or else face the enforcement consequences flowing from disobedience. If my Albanian-born driver had sped at 70 mph to spirit me to LaGuardia Airport, he could have been pulled over and given a traffic ticket by one of New York's finest. My Balkan friend would have violated the appropriately dubbed speed "limits."

RECOGNIZING THE HIGHER LAW

Obedience to law does not mean that laws must be blindly accepted and slavishly followed, regardless of their effects on freedom. After all, ours is a constitutional republic. That means, even from a secular perspective, that a higher law exists and that higher law is the Constitution of the United States. In practical effect, a law duly passed by Congress and signed into law by the president may exceed the powers granted to the federal government under our Constitution. Or, a law enacted through that same constitutionally ordained process may impermissibly tromp all over the individual rights guaranteed to Americans by the Bill of Rights.

How? Two examples illustrate the point.

Imagine a law that brings about a federal takeover of the entire public educational system in our country. Not simply regulation of public education, but an actual takeover. Under this hypothetically sweeping federal law, public schools would now be "national" schools under the direct control of the federal Department of Education and its regional offices. Such an unprecedented and extreme measure would raise issues of "federalism," which recognizes the authority of the fifty states to manage their own affairs.

Traditionally in this country, each state has been responsible for organizing and overseeing its elementary and secondary education systems. Ditto for colleges. The national government has control of the military academies, but the proud Wolverines of the University of Michigan, for example, are governed by a state-controlled board. Likewise, state law delegates and empowers local school boards to create and administer the public schools in their respective districts. In my community of Waco, TX, for instance, no less than four independent school districts are located within a fifteen-minute drive of our house. Each of the four districts has an elected school board whose membership is comprised of unpaid citizen-volunteers.

Our highly decentralized educational structure demonstrates the following reality: Americans want local control of their schools, subject, of course, to state and federal regulation. We would not readily accept a federal takeover of what is, historically, a state and local function. Nor would a state takeover of local public schools be blithely accepted outside of extraordinary circumstances, such as a community school being placed in some form of "receivership."

Consider a second example—a federal law that violates our individual liberties. Such a law was passed in violation of the Bill of Rights early on in our country's history. In practical effect, the Alien and Sedition Laws of 1798 prohibited criticism of the federal government, beginning with the president himself. Criticize John Adams and you could land in jail. Some poor souls met that very fate.

These laws were horribly unconstitutional and constituted flagrant violations of the freedoms of speech and press protected by the First Amendment. Eventually repealed by Congress (after Thomas Jefferson took office), the laws were jettisoned before the Supreme Court had the opportunity to strike them down as unconstitutional. But rest assured, they didn't pass the constitutional smell test.

These extreme examples—one hypothetical, one real—illustrate the broader point that though questionable laws may well find their way into the law books, at some juncture they will be subject to a higher law—that of America's Constitution, including its Bill of Rights.

In this book, we're not simply exploring general issues of federalism or personal liberties, though those will arise. Here, we're looking at a particular issue of liberty—religious liberty. As we explore together critical issues of religious freedom in America, we bear in mind that "the blessings of liberty," as outlined in the Preamble to the Constitution, are secured ultimately by fidelity to our higher law.

But how do we know what the higher law commands when it comes to religious liberty? When does the nation's ultimate law—the Constitution and the twenty-seven amendments to the original document—rise up in righteous indignation and invalidate a "lower" law passed by Congress, a state legislature, or a local government? When is a president's power constrained as falling beyond the constitutional limits of presidential authority? These questions invite us into the chambers of the third branch of the federal government, the United States Supreme Court. Our first stop in Constitution Hall, so to speak, is a room marked (figuratively speaking), "Caesar, Do Not Enter." We examine our Constitution in action, giving practical meaning in everyday life to "liberty" under law.

Let's begin the journey.

— I —

HANDS OFF, CAESAR!

I n the second week of March 2020, I was in New York City to film *Firing Line*, the television show created by one of my heroes, the late William F. Buckley, Jr. It was to be a quick trip, in and out. From there, I was to fly to Denver for a daylong set of presentations at Colorado Christian University in suburban Lakewood.

Like everyone else, I was tracking the news. A new virus was spreading across the globe. Still, no recordings or speaking events had been canceled. No one in the airports or on the streets was wearing face masks. No lockdown orders had been issued. It was another day in a now foregone era, the era before COVID-19 changed everything.

In the early hours of that morning, I made my way to the Empire Hotel gym across from Lincoln Center for a preshow workout. I looked around that small room, hoping to find sanitary wipes. Seeing none and aware of the growing threat of the coronavirus to those my age, I left the gym, informed the night clerk of the need for new wipes, and opted for a walk outside in America's most exciting city.

There was a nervous energy as I walked through the city. There were fewer people on the streets, and those who'd ventured out kept their heads down. Everyone seemed to avoid each other. A few wore masks before it was *en vogue*. The people had already gotten the message. Within hours, Governor Andrew Cuomo announced a statewide lockdown.

I think about my last stroll through New York City more and more these days. Aware of the growing threat, I made a choice and took my exercise the old-fashioned way—a vigorous walk in the bracing weather of early March—instead of subjecting myself to any number of viruses that might have been haunting the gym.

The people of New York City were already making their choices, too. They were huddled up in their homes. But within mere days of that brisk walk, our choices evaporated. Gyms across the country closed at the instruction of state and local governments. Shelter-in-place and social-distancing orders quickly became routine, while governors and mayors stepped into leadership roles ordinarily associated with a local or regional natural disaster, such as a hurricane. In those roles, they asked hard questions: Which businesses had to close? What services were essential? Could worship services continue?

As lockdown orders rolled out, different states (and sometimes cities within those states) fashioned different approaches. Business closures and layoffs cascaded across the country at unprecedented levels. Unemployment skyrocketed to levels not seen since the Great Depression. The human and economic wreckage was appalling.

What's more, churches were not shielded from the onslaught, nor were religiously affiliated institutions. Many state and local governing authorities significantly limited, or outright banned, worship services. As a result, church giving declined. In some places, the falloff in giving was so significant that church staff had to be reduced. Religion, just like virtually every other sector of American society, other than Walmart and the local liquor stores, was facing a deep crisis.

FAITH IN LOCKDOWN: RELIGIOUS LIBERTY IN THE CORONAVIRUS AGE

In the book of Matthew, the opponents of Jesus came with a question: Was it lawful for a God-fearing Jew to pay taxes to Caesar? You may remember Jesus's answer. He asked one of these opponents to produce a Roman coin, then inquired: "Whose face is on the coin?" When his interrogator answered, "Caesar's," Jesus answered, "Render to Caesar the things that are Caesar's, and to God the things that are God's."

What did Jesus mean? Interpreting the Messiah can be a tricky business, but I believe he meant that governments have certain powers in this world, and we should honor and respect those powers.

But what happens when Caesar's orders conflict with religious faith and practice? What happens when, for instance, Caesar's orders create a crisis of belief in the middle of a health crisis? Who wins?

Perhaps a better question is this: who should win, particularly in a country in which the Constitution seems by its very words to prohibit government meddling with faith?

What do I mean?

Let's recall the text of the First Amendment to the United States Constitution:

> Congress shall make no law respecting an establishment of religion, or prohibiting the free exercise thereof; or abridging the freedom of speech, or of the press; or the right of the people peaceably to assemble, and to petition the government for a redress of grievances.

Baked into that amendment are the bedrock rights of America: to believe as you will; to express those beliefs; and to assemble with those who are like-minded, all without government intrusion.

This clause, often known as the establishment clause, is a significant check on the government. But in the face of the twenty-first century COVID-19 pandemic, a very large number of American Caesars—mostly governors and city mayors—have seemed to run afoul of this clause. How?

Living through the COVID lockdowns, we are vividly aware of the closure of houses of worship while other "essential businesses" are allowed to remain open. In Missouri, citizens could only attend places of worship if no more than ten people were present, but liquor stores remained open to the public.[1] In California, citizens were prohibited from attending church services while marijuana dispensaries were considered "essential businesses" and allowed to sell recreational weed.[2]

In Nevada, the Governor issued an astonishing order that in

effect shut down worship services, but allowed casinos to operate. The case made its way to the Supreme Court on an emergency basis, but to no avail. The nation's highest court allowed, strangely, this disparity to continue. Objecting vehemently to this church vs. casino dichotomy, Justice Gorsuch excoriated the five-member Court majority's turning a blind eye to the outrage: "[T]here is no world in which the Constitution permits Nevada to favor Caesars Palace over Calvary Chapel."

TO RESIST OR COMPLY?
THAT IS THE QUESTION

In New York City, which bore the brunt of the first wave of the pandemic, faith communities obeyed the mayor's stay-at-home orders. But compliance with similar orders across the country was even more noteworthy since many communities were largely spared the first wave of the horrific pandemic impact.

Still, informed that large gatherings created settings where the virus could spread with astonishing speed, and believing the government's specific warnings, people of faith went along with Caesar's directives. Zoom, a video-conferencing platform, became a necessary ministry tool. Online worship services became the "new normal" for the faithful. Some churches were even more creative.

Paul Daugherty, lead pastor of the 13,000-member Victory Church in Tulsa, OK, preached to thousands of congregants on a regular basis, but as the pandemic took hold and lockdown orders went into effect, he had an idea. He could comply with Caesar's orders and still speak to his people in the flesh. So, he opened the parking lot for the congregants' vehicles and, elevated on a scissor lift thirty feet in the air, he conducted a drive-in worship service. The praise team led music from the church roof and when the music stopped, he preached from his lofty perch.

The resulting worship experience was inspirational, with joy-filled Victory Church worshipers honking their horns in a benedictory response of gratitude. What's more, the service was carried live on a local FM station and livestreamed to more than 120,000 souls who saved gas money and remained safely at home.

Here's the part of this story that has been often overlooked. Pastor Daugherty sought and received preclearance from Tulsa's mayor to conduct the service. It was a small act with large significance. The country had entered a new era; an era in which Caesar had to be consulted in advance of holding worship services.

Victory Church's innovations were mirrored across the nation, as countless houses of faith sincerely sought to comply with official directives and Center for Disease Control guidelines.

But not all were quite so compliant. In fact, there were loud exceptions.

At The River Church in Tampa, FL, megachurch pastor Rodney Howard-Browne continued services as usual. The result? He was arrested for holding services in defiance of local government orders and charged with both "unlawful assembly" and "violation of a public health emergency order."[3] It was a move that did not sit well with everyone.

Pastor Howard-Browne's attorney, Liberty Counsel's Mat Staver, attacked the criminal charges, noting that The River Church had taken extra precautions and went "above and beyond" the six-foot social distancing restriction. Law enforcement's rigid approach failed to take those ameliorating factors into account, the lawyer maintained, which would likely have doomed officialdom's efforts on judicial challenge. This doubtless influenced officials' decision to dismiss the ill-conceived charges.

Similarly, at Life Tabernacle Church in Baton Rouge, LA, Pastor Tony Spell defied Governor John Bel Edwards's order banning more than fifty people gathering together. "We have a constitutional right to congregate. We will continue," he said. Drawing the battle lines, Pastor Spell emphasized that Life Tabernacle had implemented highly rigorous protective measures, boasting that it was a lot "cleaner" at Life Tabernacle than at Walmart or local gas stations which remained open for business.

The opinions regarding whether religious services should be

held during a public health crisis may vary. You may believe seeking government approval before congregating is wise. You might believe civil disobedience is in order when the government issues a "do not assemble together" order. You may believe you should keep your head down, obey the authorities, and pray. But for all the varied and frequently conflicting responses of church communities in coping with the COVID-19 crisis, people of faith should be asking one common question: when does the government's authority trump religious assembly and expression?

AUTONOMY:
THE KEY TO RELIGIOUS LIBERTY

The COVID-19 crisis shines a bright spotlight on an important concept at the heart of religious liberty in America: the autonomy principle.

Autonomy. This is a special concept for friends of religious liberty. It is one of what we can call the Great Principles that undergird our system of ordered liberty. Properly understood, the autonomy principle provides an extra layer of constitutional protection for all faith communities, and it is one that the Supreme Court has vigorously policed and guaranteed.

How does it do so? Pay attention. You might need to know your rights in these odd times of the "new normal."

Simply defined, the word "autonomy" relates to the ability to govern oneself. Put another way, autonomous individuals or organizations might say: "Leave me alone. I'm in charge of my (or our) own destiny." Autonomy is the very bedrock guaranty of religious liberty and it is a fundamental guaranty for any free individual or institution, especially churches.

Throughout our nation's history, the idea of autonomy, of leaving churches alone to govern their own affairs, has been deemed fundamental to our constitutional order. Simply put, faith-bearing Americans have upheld the notion that Caesar should mind his own business and stay out of matters of religion, including matters of church governance. This allows the faithful to freely exercise the tenets of their religion without fear of government interference, or of discrimination—a founding principle of our constitutional order.

Obviously, extreme examples demonstrate that rare exceptions may arise to the general rule. Government may have to intervene in the most exceptional circumstances to serve an overarching, powerful goal in promoting the public good. Is the outbreak of a pandemic one such example? Before we answer that question, let's delve a little deeper. Let's consider a hypothetical.

An unthinkable example is illustrative for purposes of understanding the principle. Consider human sacrifice as a ritual act of worship (which is and obviously should be a criminal act). In the event any religious group attempted to go through with such a macabre ceremony, the government would rightly step in to protect human life, even if the would-be "victim" of the ritual freely agreed to the life-ending ritual. Or, more realistically, consider possible claims of child abuse in a church school program. Once again, law enforcement or social services officials should intervene to protect the young and vulnerable.

In these hypothetical situations, the government has a "compelling" reason to intervene in religious institutions, and this laudable governmental goal provides the compelling reason for interfering with religious liberty. But extreme examples and public health emergencies aside, when viewed properly, the First Amendment does not so much create a "wall of separation" between the church and the state, but rather a "wall of protection" so that faith communities can freely chart their own course without disrupting significant public interests.

What does this look like practically speaking? Consider the rather exotic South Florida faith community of the Church of the Lukumi Babalu Aye. This is a real case, not a hypothetical.

As part of its worship services, the church engaged in the ritual sacrifice of animals. The City of Hialeah tried to put a stop to the practice by adopting an ordinance that expressed its "great concern regarding the possibility of public ritualistic animal sacrifices," before banning the practice altogether.

The ordinance did not advance a compelling government interest, at least not one that justified its effect on religious practice. What's more, the ordinance was not neutral in nature. It did not prohibit the slaughtering of chickens or cattle at a meatpacking plant.

Instead, it specifically targeted ritualistic religious sacrifices. By aiming at religious ceremonies rather than more generally outlawing the slaughtering of animals, the Supreme Court concluded that the city had violated the Constitution. It had run afoul of the implicit "non-discrimination principle" embedded in the First Amendment, and overtly threatened the autonomy of a religious organization to express its faith, even if that faith included what the community considered highly offensive rituals.

THERE'S MORE TO AUTONOMY THAN RITUALISTIC SACRIFICE

Exotica aside, we see the same great principle of autonomy at work in a case decided years later, one which pitted the civil rights forces of the Obama administration against a religious school.[4]

A Michigan Lutheran school, Hosanna-Tabor, employed Cheryl Perich to teach various secular subjects, though she also led her students in daily prayer and devotional exercises. She accompanied her students to a weekly school-wide chapel service and led the school chapel service herself twice a year. In addition, Ms. Perich had accepted a formal "call" from the congregation and became a "Minister of Religion," receiving a "diploma of vocation." This special designation separated Ms. Perich from the other, catch-all category of "lay" teachers, which was her own classification when she first entered Hosanna-Tabor's teaching ranks.

After five years of service, Cheryl Perich became ill. As court proceedings would later detail, her "symptoms included sudden and deep sleep from which she could not be roused." Her malady was eventually diagnosed as narcolepsy, a serious medical condition that is totally disabling for a classroom teacher.

Ms. Perich began the 2004-2005 academic year on disability leave, but in January 2005 she notified Hosanna-Tabor's principal that she had recovered and would be able to resume her teaching duties the following month. Unfortunately for Ms. Perich, school administrators had hired a temporary teacher to fill her position for the remainder of that school year. Even more worrisome, the principal expressed concern that Ms. Perich was not yet ready to return to the classroom despite medical clearance.

Ms. Perich insisted that she was fully recovered and entirely capable of resuming her duties. She showed up at school on the first day the doctors cleared her for work, but school administrators turned her away.

From there, things went quickly downhill. Ms. Perich reached out to an attorney and informed school authorities that she intended to assert her legal rights. Though this was entirely permissible from a legal standpoint, in the context of Hosanna-Tabor's theology (they believed Christians should not sue other Christians) this was an unpardonable sin. For this offense, and for conduct more generally considered as insubordination, Ms. Perich was fired.

She filed a charge with the Equal Employment Opportunity Commission (EEOC) claiming her employment had been terminated in violation of the Americans with Disabilities Act, a federal law prohibiting an employer from discriminating against a qualified individual on the basis of disability. Her claim was weighty. After all, she overcame her job-threatening illness and was medically cleared and eager to return to her duties; yet, the school insisted that she wasn't really cured.

Even worse from a legal perspective, under federal law the school had fired her for filing a complaint with the federal civil rights agency. Though that termination was consistent with the school's theological beliefs—Paul instructed the believers in Corinth to avoid suits with one another (1 Cor. 6:1-8)—the teacher's termination constituted an act of "retaliation," which was specifically prohibited by federal civil rights laws.

The facts seemed bleak, but the federal trial court ruled in favor of Hosanna-Tabor, applying a "ministerial exception." What was the ministerial exception? It was a religious-based carve out to civil rights laws created by courts (not by Congress) that protected churches from being sued for discrimination by their ministers and teachers, particularly if those ministers or teachers were fired for theological reasons.

Ms. Perich appealed the case, and the Sixth Circuit Court of Appeals concluded that Ms. Perich was simply teaching the same secular subjects she'd taught prior to being "called" by the church to her "vocation;" therefore, the "ministerial exception" didn't apply to Hosanna-Tabor's actions. In plain English, Ms. Perich's claims for retaliatory termination could move forward in the trial court.

The case was sent back down to the lower court for trial and after years of legal wrangling the Supreme Court eventually took up the case. In a far-reaching opinion by Chief Justice John Roberts, the court applied the Great Principle of autonomy and vindicated Hosanna-Tabor's prerogative to hire and fire its teachers, as well as members of the clergy.

What's more, the Obama-era EEOC, which pressed the case to the nation's highest court, did not garner a single favorable vote from the nine justices, not even from progressive Justice Ruth Bader Ginsburg (the "Notorious RBG") or either of President Obama's appointees, Justices Sonia Sotomayor and Elena Kagan.

It was an astounding case, one in which the nine justices set aside their usual ideological differences and rallied around the flag of religious freedom for faith-based institutions. In a memorable passage from the opinion, the nation's seventeenth chief justice wrote: "By imposing an unwanted minister, the state infringes the free exercise clause, which protects a religious group's right to shape its own faith and mission through its appointments."[5]

Could there be a clearer assertion of the principle of autonomy? For good measure, the Chief Justice Roberts continued: "According the state the power to determine which individuals will minister to the faithful also violates the establishment clause, which prohibits government involvement in such ecclesiastical decisions."[6]

President Obama's EEOC had terribly miscalculated. As the secularists in that powerful federal agency mistakenly saw it, Hosanna-Tabor enjoyed only the same bundle of rights as, say, the Rotary Club or the Boy Scouts, i.e., the freedom to associate with one another, but nothing more. Remarkably, that belief was applied against Hosanna-Tabor in a virulently anti-faith way. The result? The secularists who dominated the Obama-era EEOC failed in spectacular fashion.

In its opinion, the Supreme Court explained that the First Amendment provides a special sort of solicitude for the prerogatives of religious organizations. Churches and church-connected schools were totally distinct from organizations like the Lions Club or the Chamber of Commerce. The former (churches), but not the latter (secular organizations), were given the shield of constitutionally guaranteed autonomy that was far more protective than the rights of association in a free society.

It is notable that Justices Samuel Alito and Elena Kagan, two jurists who are frequently at odds, joined forces in a concurring opinion giving wide berth to institutional autonomy. Speaking for them both, Justice Alito wrote: "Religious autonomy means that religious authorities must be free to determine who is qualified to serve in positions of substantial religious importance."[7]

What did all this mean?

To put it bluntly, religious institutions could engage in otherwise-forbidden acts of discrimination against its clergy and teachers of the faith yet entirely avoid accountability to the government. The Supreme Court had unanimously sent this message loud and clear: "Caesar, keep your hands off of religious institutions' hiring and firing decisions."

WHAT DOES THIS MEAN FOR PEOPLE OF FAITH IN TIMES OF CRISIS?

In an era of government overreach, what principles can we extract from these two Supreme Court decisions concerning the City of Hialeah and Hosanna-Tabor? From these cases we learn that, absent compelling reasons, the government cannot pass laws that target religious institutions in discriminatory ways; and governmental entities cannot interfere with religious institutions, including church schools, in ways that compromise their autonomy to express their beliefs and carry out their faith vision.

If these bedrock principles are not upheld, if authorities are allowed to run afoul of them, the powerful assurance provided by America's "first freedom," the freedom of religious liberty, will be in jeopardy.

Will the Supreme Court continue along this freedom-ensuring course in the days to come? That is a particularly pressing issue now. In an age of deepening hostility toward religious faith where some government actors seem to use any crisis, including a public health crisis, as a pretext to single out religious gatherings, will the Supreme Court step in?

As we'll explore in this book, the prospects for continuing protection of religious liberty are actually quite good. Still, if we are to maintain our religious freedoms in America, we must be willing to stand up against laws and regulations that threaten to compromise their autonomy.

So, if the pattern of laws in your state or community target religious practice, if the government challenges the autonomy of the institution without a compelling reason, consider your recourse. You might choose to obey the ruling authorities, as Paul instructs in his letter to the Romans, and give up your rights, (Rom. 13:1). Or, you can follow Paul's example and litigate to the hilt, including appealing to Caesar.

If you know your rights, if you understand the constitutional constraints placed on government when it comes to religious liberty, you'll be ready to fight when the time is right. You'll know how and when to act when the next crisis comes calling. And, make no mistake about it, the next crisis is coming.

How do I know? History is our wise teacher. That being so, let's march down Memory Lane and examine the place of history and tradition (another Great Principle of freedom) in America's framework of religious liberty.

— 2 —

FAITH OF OUR FATHERS

From an early age, we are taught to respect our elders. For those of us hailing from the Judeo-Christian background, this teaching is rooted in the fifth commandment to honor our fathers and mothers. It is, after all, "the first commandment with promise," with the ancient text indicating that adherence to the command will lead to long life.

If we are obedient to our parents, if our parents were obedient to our grandparents, and our grandparents likewise to their parents (and so on), we might see an impressive march of many generations, extending far back in the corridors of time.

Obedience as children is not the only way to honor our parents. We "honor" our parents as adults through setting aside special days to celebrate them—Mother's Day and Father's Day—and giving them meaningful gifts on their birthdays and at Christmas.

But "honors" don't stop at the front door. As a society, we go far beyond the family circle and honor the lives of our forefathers and those who came after them. We set aside special days for our entire country such as Thanksgiving (in both the United States and Canada) and perhaps above all here in the USA, the Fourth of July, the nation's birthday.

We celebrate special birthdays, too; that of Dr. Martin Luther King, Jr. in January, and Presidents' Day in February, as we remember the magnificent contributions of George Washington and Abraham

Lincoln. Memorial Day comes in May, when we honor our fallen soldiers, and then Veterans Day in November. We remember workers on Labor Day as summer vacations draw to a close.

With these nationwide honor-bestowing salutes, we are affirming something particular. That is, we come from a particular people with particular traditions, and these people and traditions are important. They touch our hearts. These days of national remembrance and celebration bind us together as a free people. They are unifiers, and they are all the more important in our age of deep cultural and political divisions.[1]

How we choose to honor a specific person or a certain event is shaped in no small part by the culture of the day, and by our shared experiences over time. Though cultural influences abound, throughout American history our national experience has been inexorably shaped by religion, and expressly, by Christianity.

Again, we think of Dr. King, and his magnificent "Letter from a Birmingham Jail." That mighty missive was an unapologetically Christian call for justice, even when calling for the exercise of conscience to commit nonviolent acts of civil disobedience. Any attempt to remove Christianity from the celebration of Dr. King's writings and his life would be nothing short of dishonor.

At times, we honor our forefathers and the events that shaped our history with symbols of shared cultural values, often in the form of memorials and monuments. That's what happened in a suburb of our nation's capital in the wake of World War I.

THE CROSS: HISTORICAL SYMBOL OR A CONSTITUTIONAL VIOLATION?

No one alive in this third decade of the twenty-first century experienced what our great grandparents called the Great War. The entire world, it seemed, was indeed at war even though the theaters of battle were centered on the European continent. Approximately 40 million soldiers and civilians died in World War I, including more than 100,000 American soldiers. Their sacrifice was deemed necessary, as the Great War was boldly considered to be the war to end all wars.

I remember the sadness of "reading along" with our daughter, Carolyn (now the mother of her own four wonderful children) when she was a sophomore in college. For a special project, she poured herself into an elaborately researched and wonderfully written book, *The Pity of War*, by historian Niall Ferguson. It was my first deep dive into a largely forgotten war and, as I read, I found the book was aptly named since its horrific loss of life was indeed a pity and a human tragedy of epic proportions.

Guiding us into the Great War with idealism and optimism, President Woodrow Wilson knew that American firepower would likely prove decisive. It did, but at horrific cost of lost lives of the nation's young men (women were not permitted to serve in combat roles until a century later). Among the dead were forty-nine young men who hailed from Prince George's County in Maryland, situated just across the line from the District of Columbia.

At the conclusion of the war, a question arose. How should communities honor those who never returned, some of whom had found their final resting place on foreign soil? As cultural practices developed, military cemeteries began erecting crosses and Stars of David over the graves of Christian and Jewish soldiers respectively. Even as recently as the Spanish-American War of 1898, this had not been the practice. In fact, by military tradition, the gravestones of fallen soldiers were rectangular and devoid of religious symbolism. But the Great War changed everything, introducing religious symbolism into military cemeteries throughout Europe.

The war officially ended on November 11, 1918, which became known as Armistice Day. After the armistice agreement was signed, the Department of Defense (then known as the War Department) announced plans to replace the wooden crosses and Stars of David with the rather nondescript, uniform marble slabs traditionally used in military cemeteries. Tellingly, the public outcry was loud and clear: "Don't do that, War Department!" The American people did not want the gravesites of their sons, who were buried under the precious symbols of the cross and Stars of David, to be desecrated by bureaucrats. They could not countenance the religious symbols being removed and replaced with emotionless concrete slabs devoid of spiritual meaning.

In that cultural moment, the citizenry of Bladensburg, MD, a proud city in Prince George's County, rallied together and organized a committee for the purpose of erecting a memorial to honor the county's fallen soldiers. Ten mothers of soldiers killed on foreign soil served as key members of the organizing committee. Early on, the memorial committee decided that the war monument should be in the form of a cross. A sculptor was hired, fundraising efforts got under way, and the project was off and running.

In its effort to raise funds, the committee crafted the following message to the community: "We, the citizens of Maryland, trusting in God, the Supreme Ruler of the Universe, Pledge Faith in our Brothers who gave their all in the World War to make the World Safe for Democracy." The project's stated cause was entirely political and secular in nature, to make the world "safe for democracy." The fundraising message continued: "With our Motto, 'One God, One Country, and One Flag' We contribute to this Memorial Cross Commemorating the Memory of those who have not Died in Vain."

With funds in hand, the community gathered for the groundbreaking ceremony in September 1919. The mother of the first Prince George's County resident killed in Europe was selected to break ground. However, fundraising efforts soon faltered, even with the support of the county's business and political leaders and construction was halted. The local post of the American Legion then stepped in, provided the necessary resources to get construction going again, and the monument was finally completed several years later in 1925.

It was a long process. The Bladensburg Cross project represented a quintessentially American, community-led effort.

The monument is impressive. The Latin cross is thirty-two feet high, sitting atop a large pedestal. On the pedestal are inscribed four words: Valor, Endurance, Courage, and Devotion. At the center of the pedestal is the emblem of the sponsoring organization, the American Legion. Adorning the pedestal is a large bronze plaque with this inscription: "Dedicated to the heroes of Prince George's County, Maryland, who lost their lives in the Great War for the liberty of the world." The plaque then identifies by name the forty-nine sons of Prince George's County who died in combat.

The background and context make clear that the Bladensburg Cross was not a church project. It was not erected by a religious order as a call to the faithful. Far from it. It was a citizens' project, born in the ineffable sadness captured in Niall Ferguson's poignant description "the pity of war." Young men had died, and many had been buried in foreign lands. Their youthful European military adventure had ended tragically, captured in John McCrae's poem "In Flanders Fields," this way:

In Flanders fields the poppies blow
Between the crosses row on row.

The words set forth on the plaque were deeply human—qualities such as valor are by no means peculiar to religious life. What's more, no quotations from scripture found their way onto the plaque or anywhere else on the memorial cross. It was, rather, an enormous version of a tombstone, without the mortal remains of a brave soldier resting underneath.

It was the citizens' expression of commitment to an earthly cause— to protect democracy—and to honor all of the county's sons who had perished overseas. The mother of one fallen soldier expressed the sentiment this way: "The chief reason that I feel this way [in supporting the project] is that my son [...] lost his life in France and because [...] our memorial cross is, in a way, his gravestone."

For decades, the uncontroversial memorial cross stood on what became, over time, public land. Prince George's County grew, transforming itself into a suburb of Washington, DC, and Bladensburg became a bustling crossroads. Eventually, the memorial cross was transferred to the local government in Bladensburg and maintained thereafter by a state-appointed commission.

As the years went by, the Bladensburg Cross found itself at the center of a busy intersection. Its towering height and enviably pivotal location meant that, as a practical matter, the eyes of drivers and passengers alike could not be turned away from the memorial cross. Even more relevantly, the culture of the community changed. Emerging from the shadows in the twenty-first century was the American Humanist Association (we'll call them the Humanists), a secular organization dedicated to a nonreligious, nontheistic world view.

And so, the lawsuit began. The idea undergirding the legal challenge was simple: the Bladensburg Cross, albeit a war memorial, was a religious symbol, the Humanists claimed. The government, so the argument went, could not support or maintain this ultimate expression of the Christian faith. In constitutional parlance, the memorial cross embodied an "establishment" of religion. As the foundational symbol of Christianity, the Bladensburg Cross had to be torn down, or else dramatically reconfigured, to eliminate the inarguably religious nature of the symbol.

The Humanists hit pay dirt. Although a federal district judge in Maryland rebuffed the constitutional challenge, the United States Court of Appeals for the Fourth Circuit, headquartered in Richmond, VA, agreed with the Humanists. The court found that the memorial cross was an unacceptable symbol of Christianity physically situated on public property. It had to come down, or at least some alternative arrangement had to be made, such as moving the memorial physically, or transferring ownership of the property (and the cross) to a private foundation.

Were the appellate judges just evincing a hostility to religion in general, or to Christianity in particular? Perhaps, though it can be difficult to know any judge's deepest thoughts in coming to his or her ultimate decision with respect to the Constitution's meaning. Still, I do not think the Fourth Circuit judges were demonstrating a hostility to religion, because I consider them judges at their word. Here, the judges who concluded that the memorial cross violated America's Constitution, specifically the establishment clause of the First Amendment, had before them a long line of aging Supreme Court cases that, fairly read, called the memorial cross into question.

Which cases?

One extraordinarily influential Supreme Court decision, *Lemon v. Kurtzman*, proved to be a mighty engine of destruction when antireligious groups such as the Humanists took control of the litigation wheel. The constitutional doctrine emerging in that case, which was decided in 1971, demanded that any challenged governmental action relating to religion, such as the maintenance of the memorial cross, must have a primarily secular purpose and secular effect. Certainly, fair-minded judges could readily conclude that the ultimate symbol of the Christian faith, the cross, could not be viewed as anything other than a governmental embrace of America's majority faith.

Why else would a heavily trafficked public space feature a cross?

It was the *Lemon* decision that sounded (temporarily) the death knell for the memorial cross, but that fatal bell sounded only in Richmond, VA, in the federal appellate court. The case was taken up to the United States Supreme Court, which stepped into the fray and struck a powerful blow in favor of history and tradition.[2]

In a stunning 7-2 decision, the Supreme Court concluded that the Bladensburg Cross would continue to stand. The basis of the court's decision? The cross was not so much a religious symbol as it was a monument to history and tradition, reflecting and embodying the culture of the people who erected it.

All but two of the nine justices (Justice Ginsburg and Justice Sotomayor, who viewed the monument as a religious statement) accepted that proposition, determining that the long-standing religious symbol could remain in place on public land, maintained and preserved through the expenditure of local taxpayer dollars.

To say it was a blow to the Humanists is an understatement.

Because you are reading this book, I'd guess your reaction to be something akin to this:

"Good riddance to the mean-spirited Humanists! After all, the memorial cross had been standing for nearly ninety years before they launched their audacious and ill-fated legal challenge. They shouldn't have waited so long to head into court. After all, the law frequently imposes time limits to cut off litigation when the underlying event being complained of—say, an automobile accident—occurred many years earlier."

Fair point. But that commonsense rationale provided no basis for tossing the Humanists' lawsuit. Why? Because if a practice violates the Constitution, it doesn't earn some blanket of immunity by virtue of its longevity.

In the world of cultural practices and the Constitution, though, ripe age can vindicate a practice that might otherwise be vulnerable to judicial challenge.[2] To demonstrate the validating nature of history and tradition, the Supreme Court in the *Bladensburg Cross* case looked by way of analogy to the commonplace practice of featuring the Ten Commandments in public places. The profound religious significance of the Decalogue is undeniable. Yet, the commandments handed down to Moses on Mount Sinai are featured in numerous public buildings, including the Supreme Court building itself. That is, this sacred text has taken on historical significance to society in a more general, nonreligious sense. True, the Ten Commandments stand not only as sacred text, but also as culture-shaping principles guiding the formation of laws that bind us all, regardless of our faith journey (or lack of one).

Writing for the seven-member majority favoring the Bladensburg Cross, Justice Samuel Alito took on the role of history professor. How had the Ten Commandments become so frequently found across the American landscape, finding their way onto such public places as state capitol grounds?

The story, briefly told, began with a state judge in Minnesota in 1946 who was deeply concerned about what he saw as an exploding growth in juvenile delinquency. His suggested response was to create public displays of the Ten Commandments to remind young people of the community's governing principles.

The idea quickly gained adherents, attracting the enthusiastic attention of then Hollywood mogul, Cecil B. DeMille. The promoter of large stories for the silver screen, DeMille tied his production of a blockbuster movie by that name, *The Ten Commandments*, with the growing nationwide civic effort to display the Decalogue.

With that background, as Justice Alito saw it, the cultural movement favoring displaying the Ten Commandments on various monuments and memorials was motivated by societal concerns, in particular the perceived decline in morality among the nation's youth. It was not part of a back-to-church initiative. It was part of a culture-shaping initiative.

Justice Alito delved into sociology. Monuments and memorials, in time, take on a secondary meaning. The tragic fires that engulfed Notre Dame Cathedral in Paris rallied the people of France, he noted. Notre Dame was not only a sacred place of worship; it had become a primary symbol of the French nation.

Similarly, the iconic Statue of Liberty "began as a monument to the solidarity and friendship between France and the United States and only decades later came to be seen 'as a beacon welcoming immigrants to a land of freedom.'"[3] With the passage of time, the court emphasized, monuments and symbols, including religious ones, can "become embedded features of a community's landscape and identity."[4]

Especially important in the court's calculus was its concern about the perception of governmental hostility to religion. In fact, one of the Fourth Circuit judges had suggested the Bladensburg Cross could remain so long as the two arms should be sawed off.

This appallingly insensitive idea not only drew a sharp rebuke from the Supreme Court, it prompted an important statement about the place of religion in a pluralistic society. Namely, the Supreme Court warned that sweeping across the land, tearing down monuments, renaming cities (say, Corpus Christi here in my home state of Texas), and otherwise seeking to "de-Christianize" American society would reasonably be perceived as governmental hostility to religion. In fact, contemporary cultural movements to tear down monuments such as those of Confederate generals are undertaken precisely because the values embodied by those monuments are deemed inimical to the values of twenty-first century America.

A governmental jihad against historical monuments bearing any nexus to religion would naturally be seen as the constitutionally impermissible opposite of "establishing" a church. It would signal a war against religion, and particularly the majority religion whose symbols traditionally reflected American culture. That would not do, and the majority of the court made sure of it.

The Bladensburg Cross was safe and secure.

LEGISLATIVE PRAYER CONFRONTS THE ESTABLISHMENT CLAUSE

But what about prayer? Specifically, what about those kinds of prayers that have always been a part of our national institutions? Unlike monuments and memorials such as the Bladensburg Cross, there's no getting around the fact that prayer is quintessentially a religious act. Neither sociological analysis nor cultural wrangling can free us from that reality.

Memorial crosses may adorn time-honored monuments, and they may enshrine a certain cultural moment, but a prayer is here and now. Therefore, can the courts justify Congressional practices like hiring chaplains, paying them out of public funds, and allowing clerics to take the podium and offer an invocation prior to any legislative session? (For the record, this happens at the federal level in both the House and the Senate.) The well-meaning atheist might ask: "Isn't this the very thing the establishment clause is meant to protect against?"

For friends of religious liberty, the answer to the atheist is happily, "no." Why? Because like monuments, religious belief and practice are found once again in history and tradition of our great country. For more than two centuries, the legislative-chaplain practice has prevailed and remained unchallenged for the lion's share of that long history. But as the Supreme Court began to confront establishment clause challenges more frequently during the era of Chief Justice Earl Warren (the presiding chief justice from 1953 to 1969), it seemed inevitable that courts would be asked the question on many citizens' minds.

Does the taxpayer-paid chaplaincy practice violate the establishment clause?

As so commonly happens, this establishment clause squabble arose in the context of a state, rather than a federal, practice. Specifically, a member of Nebraska's unicameral legislature—the only one in the country—filed a federal constitutional challenge to the Cornhusker State's century-long tradition. Once again, the anti-religion challenge hit paydirt. The lower federal courts concluded that the practice constituted a clear-cut violation of the establishment clause.

The result seems correct at first blush. How could it not be? Recall the sweep of the words themselves that open the Bill of Rights: "Congress shall make no law respecting an establishment of religion." Short of legislatively creating the Church of the United States (think of the Church of England), the practice of creating an official religious post complete with an impressive title "Chaplain of the Senate" (ditto for the House of Representatives), furnishing a handsome office in the Capitol building itself, and providing for a small, taxpayer-paid staff, all certainly sounds like a law "respecting" an "establishment of religion."

The words of the First Amendment seemed clear, and the Supreme Court's case law pointed in the direction of sure-fire judicial invalidation of the long practice. The pundits thought this would be a lock. The pundits and court-watchers, however, were wrong.

At the Supreme Court, the court under Chief Justice Warren Burger (who served from 1969-1985) upheld Nebraska's practice largely on the strength of what Congress had been doing from the very beginning of the republic.

Truth be told, the historical case was indeed impressive. From the First Congress forward, both the House and the Senate had paid chaplaincies. The practice developed without serious, much less sustained, opposition. The unanimity of the acceptance of the practice was illustrated by the fact that James Madison, the primary architect of the Bill of Rights, served as a member of the House committee that both approved the practice and selected the inaugural officeholder of the House chaplaincy.

But it wasn't simply the First Congress. The tradition continued year after year and, indeed, for the following several centuries of America's experiment in constitutional democracy. The practice became so engrained in both Washington, DC, and throughout the country, that five members of the court—over a stinging dissenting opinion—decided to leave it undisturbed. Legislative prayer had become a traditional part of our country's governance.

Was the court simply creating an "exception" to the rule that Congress can't pay preachers' salaries, much less hire them and give them cushy offices at the seat of government? Or, was the court interpreting the establishment clause as actively promoting (not just permitting) the idea that long-standing cultural practices could remain in place?

It was the latter.

We'll see this concept more vividly in a later chapter, but legislative prayer introduces us to a very important concept in religious liberty—accommodation. That is, even in the face of the capacious, seemingly absolutist wording of the establishment clause, its original meaning—as vividly illuminated by the practice of the First Congress—accommodated the traditional practices of legislative bodies as representatives of "We the People," the Preamble's opening words.

What history and tradition had joined together, Supreme Court doctrine would not tear asunder.

Chief Justice Burger's opinion represented the pro-religious liberty wing of the Supreme Court hard at work, eschewing the rigidity that occasionally flowed from the strict application of judicially-created doctrine or theory. Simply because of its long vintage, the practice of legislative prayer could coexist peacefully with the general prohibition against governmental "establishments" of religion.

Put another way, history and tradition, taken together, actually form a method of interpreting the Constitution.

This is not as surprising or unorthodox as it may seem at first blush. Much of what we call "constitutional law" has its origins in the actual day-to-day practice of government as it has unfolded over time.

Take the concept of separation of powers—the division of authority among the three branches of the federal government. The text of our founding document never employs the phrase "separation of powers." That's a logical inference that we draw from the text and structure of the Constitution, and it has huge implications.

What implications?

Consider our most recent presidential impeachment, and President Donald Trump's invocation of "executive privilege" to shield certain documents and witnesses. Executive privilege is likewise not mentioned in the Constitution, nor does the concept appear in the lively debates at the Constitutional Convention in Philadelphia in 1787.

But the concept of protecting the confidentiality of presidential conversations and deliberations is inherent (or implicit) in a governmental architecture of separated powers. After all, could any president serve faithfully without the assurance that Oval Office conversations with cabinet members and aides were fully protected by law? This privilege grew directly from the history and tradition of our country.

Or, consider the questions raised about the extent of presidential power to take retaliatory military action against Syria or preemptively to take out a senior military officer of the government of Iran. There is nothing directly granting these presidential authorities, but looking to history for guidance we can see that many presidents have exercised just these kinds of powers over the years. Ergo, what seems to be a challengeable action actually passes constitutional muster.

So, too, in a time of domestic crisis, such as President Trump's response to the COVID-19 pandemic. We ask the question: in seeking to resolve a constitutional challenge to presidential action, what did General Washington or Mr. Jefferson do during their respective service in the nation's highest office? How did they wield power as they responded to the crises of their time?

This diversion leads us to an important insight: the issue of the constitutionality of legislative prayer does not stand alone in the archives of constitutional interpretation. Its example, however, demonstrates the strength of our nation's history and tradition in giving concrete meaning to the constitutional text. This could not be truer than in interpreting the establishment clause.

THE PRESERVING POWER OF HISTORY AND TRADITION

The acid test of history's interpretive power came about in the second, and far more difficult, legislative prayer case involving a town council in upstate New York.

Just as the mothers of Prince George's County were the moving forces behind the Bladensburg Cross project, a citizen was the
motivating force for a new town council practice. The newly-elected
town supervisor, John Auberger, had served previously in the county
legislature, where every legislative session began in prayer.

The whimsically-named town of Greece, in contrast, customarily
began each town council meeting with a simple moment of silence.
With his fellow councilmembers in cheerful accord though, Auberger
changed the practice. As a result, local members of the clergy were
invited to deliver an invocation prior to each monthly meeting.

The clergy member would also receive the honor of being named
"Clergyman of the month," which became a sort of sought-after hon-
orific title among the ministers and pastors of Greece.

This newly-minted exercise was challenged by two townspeople
who regularly had business before the council. Among other things,
the objectors complained that the invited clergy all hailed from various
Christian denominations. Heeding the complaint, the town council
promptly shifted course, and opened the prayer-leadership opportunity
to other faith communities, including the chair of the local Baha'i
temple and a Wiccan priestess.

This considerable concession didn't satisfy the two challengers,
however, and as things often happen in America, a federal lawsuit was
filed in an attempt to halt to the new custom.

As with the Nebraska case, the lower court directed the ritual to stop.
Accepting the proposition that legislative prayer (including practices
of local town councils) was indeed permissible as a general matter,
the federal appellate court in New York concluded that any outsider
would perceive that the town council was favoring Christianity over
other faiths. So, the Second Circuit Court of Appeals in Manhattan
concluded the practice was impermissible.

The case was taken up to the Supreme Court, which once again
demonstrated the abiding power of history and tradition in establishment clause interpretation. It upheld the practice, noting that city
council invocations (even if newly introduced) were in line with the
long history and tradition of Congressional prayer. Additionally, the

practice, as it had unfolded in the town of Greece, NY, was noncoercive.

Still, the court made it abundantly clear that important boundaries remained which confined the institution of legislative prayer. Above all, the town's new practice could not be used to denigrate minority or other faith traditions, nor could it be employed deliberately to exclude certain faith communities from participation.

These two limitations demonstrated the court's keen awareness of conscientious objectors—those who took exception to government involvement in religious practices. The court held that it was vital that these objectors (and all citizens) be treated with dignity and respect, and that their worldviews and philosophies receive fair consideration.

This, too, was a deep-seated, pro-liberty value protected by America's Constitution and of fundamental importance in a free society. That is, freedom of conscience.

We turn now to examine that pivotally-important dimension of religious freedom and the Supreme Court's consistent solicitude for this foundational value in America's constitutional order.

As we will see, these two limitations concerning non-denigration and non-favoritism emerge in other arenas of religious liberty battles. In particular, we will see time and again the overarching importance of the principle that government cannot play favorites, anointing winners and denigrating "losers" in the sensitive process of framing government policy and practice.

Running afoul of this principle violates the most basic principle of freedom that each of us is free to believe.

— 3 —

FREE TO BELIEVE

Abraham Lincoln, the prairie lawyer turned "Great Emancipator," was a master of the English language. Self-taught, the future sixteenth president of the United States poured himself into two sources for his home schooling. Firstly, the collected works of William Shakespeare; secondly, the King James Version of the Bible.

But Lincoln didn't just use the Bible as a pedagogical resource. Instead, he took it to heart and applied it. As one historian put it, in his four-and-a-half years in the White House, Lincoln became "a theologian of the American idea."

Lincoln's theology of the American idea employed "the language and concepts of the Bible to reflect on the [Civil War's] larger meaning."[1] When he began his iconic remarks at Gettysburg, he invoked the language of the Bible. "Fourscore and seven years ago," echoed the elegant reflection in the Psalm, "the days of our years are threescore years and ten, and if by reason of strength they be fourscore years."[2]

As he continued his masterful address, Lincoln captured the essence of America's mission (a mission of biblical proportions) to establish liberty and equality under law. It was a mission that went so far as to abolish the abhorrent system of human slavery. It was a new vision, one which proved to be a turning point in the Civil War.

As we will see throughout this book, the core ideas of liberty and equality under the law (the Great Principles) form the foundation of so much of our legal system. From that foundation sprang the civil rights movement. From it come our notions of religious liberty, as well.

This is demonstrated nowhere better than in the Supreme Court jurisprudence of the mid-twentieth century.

Fourscore-and-ten years after Gettysburg, another self-educated lawyer, Robert Jackson, ascended to the Supreme Court bench. Like Lincoln, Jackson was born and raised "in the country." A farm boy growing up in western New York, the future attorney general and supreme court justice had limited access to formal education. He never set foot on a college campus as a student and only attended one year of law school. Again, like Lincoln, Jackson was an autodidact, immersing himself in the King James Version of the Bible and the works of Shakespeare.

In 1943, two years after ascending to the nation's highest court, Justice Jackson wrote the Supreme Court's majority opinion in *West Virginia Board of Education v. Barnette*. In that opinion, Justice Jackson crafted the words that capture the essence of the appropriate relationship between the individual and the state. Jackson wrote his opinion during another epic struggle; World War II. Just as President Lincoln in the Gettysburg Address called for a noble vision, so likewise did Jackson's *Barnette* decision.

In *Barnette*, Jackson looked past the emotion of wartime fervor and reaffirmed the fundamental right of each citizen, even schoolchildren, to live and think freely.

How?

Let's turn first to the facts of this iconic case that contributes greatly to our religious liberty landscape.

FREEDOM OF CONSCIENCE:
A MATTER OF PRINCIPLE

The Barnette sisters attended public school in rural West Virginia. Responding to the surge of patriotic sentiment during the Second World War, the West Virginia legislature passed a statute requiring all schools to teach history, civics, and "the Constitutions of the United States and [West Virginia]."³ Which was all well and good, right?

However, in early 1942, one month after the attack on Pearl Harbor, the state board of education adopted a resolution ordering a daily patriotic ceremony that included a salute to the nation's flag. Wasn't encouraging and inculcating values of patriotism and love of our nation's institutions an appropriate educational aim? Wasn't that part of our country's vitally important mission?

Indeed, it was. But the bureaucrats weren't finished. They went a step further, incorporating an unforgiving ultimatum: "[Refusal] to salute the Flag [shall] be regarded as an act of insubordination, and shall be dealt with accordingly."⁴ To make matters worse, the bureaucratic dictate included the specific form of salute—an extended right arm while the students looked up at the classroom flag.

It was too much for various groups, including the National Parent Teacher Association, the Boy Scouts and Girl Scouts, and, for good measure, the American Red Cross. The required salute, they complained, bore chilling similarity to the dreaded Nazi salute honoring Adolf Hitler.

Scrambling, the bureaucrats modified the form so that during the salute the students' palms would face upward. It was a concession, however, that did not respond to the deeper concerns animating the Barnette sisters.

The Barnette sisters came from a home of devout Jehovah's Witnesses. They, and other schoolchildren who conscientiously objected, viewed the salute to the flag (modified or otherwise) as violating God's law. To them, saluting the flag ran afoul of the Ten Commandments' injunction against bowing down to a man-made "image."

From the Jehovah's Witnesses' theological perspective, the flag was a forbidden image. According to Exodus 20:4-5: "Thou shalt not make unto thee any graven image, or likeness of anything that is in heaven above, or that is in the earth beneath, or that is in the water under the earth; thou shalt not bow down thyself to them nor serve them."⁵

Despite the objection, the West Virginia authorities brushed aside a perfectly reasonable proposed compromise, as the sisters were willing to offer the following affirmation: "I respect the flag of the United States and acknowledge it as a symbol of freedom and justice to all."[6]

That proffered version would have gone a long way to achieving the stated objective of fostering patriotic sentiments, but the schoolchildren offered more. In addition to that affirmation, they were willing, in good conscience, to recite the following pledge: "I pledge allegiance and obedience to all the laws of the United States that are consistent with God's law, as set forth in the Bible."[7]

What harm was it to the school or to the other students if the two sisters of sincere conscience quietly dissented? There would be no disruption of the ceremony, just quiet non-participation rooted in conscientious objection.

Still, the children's overtures fell flat. The state officials proved rigidly unforgiving and refused to compromise. Demonstrating once again that governmental power is all too frequently exercised unwisely (and in a fine example of what Russian novelist Fyodor Dostoyevsky called "the tyranny of the petty bureaucrat") the sisters were expelled from school.

It wasn't just the Barnette sisters, though. All throughout the Mountaineer State, children were expelled or sent home. Parents were fined and even threatened with criminal prosecution for causing juvenile delinquency. Increasingly, the state was stepping into an overweening, coercive role and the people of West Virginia were not having it. Seeking to vindicate their faith-filled stance, the Barnette family went to court.

Prospects for the schoolchildren's litigation success looked dim. Three years earlier, in 1940, the Supreme Court had upheld a similar flag-salute law that had been passed by Pennsylvania in the case of *Minersville School District v. Gobitis*. West Virginia was simply following suit with the benefit of a green light from the high court. In the schoolchildren's favor, however, was the changed judicial landscape that had resulted from President Franklin D. Roosevelt's appointment of Justice Robert H. Jackson to the Supreme Court in the year following the *Gobitis* ruling. What's more, it appeared that some of the justices were having second thoughts about *Gobitis*. Reversing course from their Keystone State decision, the court struck down the West Virginia law, concluding that forced uniformity in matters of conscience was utterly unacceptable to our constitutional order.

In essence, the court found that the Pennsylvania case from three years earlier had been wrongly decided. Why? State-initiated compulsion in matters of belief and conscience impermissibly intruded into the sacred precincts of freedom of conscience and belief. The Supreme Court had simply gotten it wrong in the earlier case. Upon further reflection and consideration, the court determined that the justices were duty bound to erase that earlier decision from the books.

It was a bold and courageous move. The justices straightforwardly acknowledged their previous error. There was no handwringing, no Hamlet-like struggling with the question: "To overrule, or not to over-rule?" Instead, the court simply did the right thing with the stroke of a pen. (Compare this, by way of example, to the court's handwringing over recent decades with respect to overruling *Roe v. Wade*. We turn more fully to this issue in Chapter 11.)

Justice Jackson set forth the court's revised thinking. In matters of patriotism and love of country, the authorities should not resort to coercion. In a passage that could readily be applied to the country's contemporary educational system, Justice Jackson noted the abysmal lack of civic education throughout the country. In his view, an edu-cated citizenry, not a coerced one, was the freedom-consistent avenue for fostering patriotism and civic pride. He wrote: "Authority here [in the United States] is to be controlled by public opinion, not public opinion by authority. [...] Compulsory unification of opinion achieves only the unanimity of the graveyard."[8]

By their rigid insistence on patriotic conformity, the West Virginia authorities had "invad[ed] the sphere of intellect and spirit which it is the purpose of the First Amendment to our Constitution to reserve from all official control."[9] Though Justice Jackson (the future chief prosecutor at the Nuremberg Trials) never said as much, the impli-cation was clear. Liberty set America apart from the coercive fascism of Hitler's Germany.

It bears noting that Justice Jackson's opinion for the court in *Barnette* did not provide refuge solely for people of faith. Rather, the safe harbor of protection from governmental coercion extended broadly to the entire range of conscientious objectors, even those not animated by a faith commitment. That breadth of freedom's reach is at the core of the *Barnette* decision's enduring strength and in no small part explains its status as one of the most hallowed decisions in American constitutional law.

Freedom from governmental coercion in matters of faith and practice is an altogether good thing. It benefits those in faith communities as well as those who don't subscribe to any faith. Freedom from coercion is not a matter of free exercise rights standing alone; it is, instead, a matter of fundamental human dignity in the face of governmental demands for conformity. Put another way, the government of the United States cannot twist your arm to espouse its own ideas.

For believers, the good news is that the elegant sweep of Justice Jackson's opinion brings under the wing of constitutional protection the entire array of human thought and contemplation. This bears emphasis. Even secularists hostile to religion can rally around the banner of *Barnette* and hail the World War II-era decision as a freedom-ensuring decision that goes to the very soul of who we are in America.

We are not a coercive nation in matters of belief. We are a nation of free belief expressed in lawful action.

THE ADVENT OF "STRICT SCRUTINY"

Concededly, Jehovah's Witness schoolchildren make an attractive category of persons deserving protection from overweening governmental action, at least as to the ideology-shaping form of compulsion. Still, the *Barnette* case ushered in a golden age of protections for freedom of conscience and belief. But the children of that minority faith are not alone.

When a devout Seventh Day Adventist, Adell Sherbert, a South Carolina textile worker, lost her job because she refused to work in the mill on Saturdays, she applied for unemployment benefits. The state denied her claim, concluding that she'd chosen not to work on her day of religious observance. Finding the decision unjust, Sherbert appealed all the way to the Supreme Court.

The court rallied to her side. As the justices saw it, state authorities were punishing her exercise of religious faith by denying her unemployment compensation. She was willing to work, the court noted, but her employer insisted she was obliged to violate her conscience by engaging in work on her Sabbath. Additionally, the state of South Carolina, by denying unemployment benefits, was tacitly supporting the employer's decision.

In contrast to the *Barnette* case, the court ruled squarely that the free exercise clause of the First Amendment required South Carolina to carve out a religion-favorable exception to its unemployment rule. Namely, if a South Carolinian suffered unemployment because he or she could not work on a day of religious observance, then that person must be guaranteed the same rights afforded to those who chose no particular day of observance.

This decision (*Sherbert v. Verner*) is another "must-know" case for friends of religious liberty. The opinion was the handiwork of the Supreme Court under the leadership of Chief Justice Earl Warren, a liberal icon. Indeed, the *Sherbert v. Verner* decision represented an about-face for Justice Warren himself, thus making the case all the more noteworthy.

As he thought through the issue of religious freedom, and in particular freedom of conscience, the chief justice from Alameda County, CA, who had once been nominated for Governor of the Golden State by both political parties, embraced a very robust view of free exercise, one different from his earlier position.

What was that previous position?

In 1961, Chief Justice Warren authored a decidedly anti-liberty opinion for the court in what came to be known as the Sunday closing cases. At the time, a number of states required businesses to be closed on Sundays in order to give the citizenry a common day of rest.

The Sunday closing measure—the very definition of governmental coercion—was challenged on various grounds, including the free exercise clause. In particular, a Philadelphia merchant, Abraham Braunfeld, complained that his Orthodox Jewish faith obliged him to close his store on Saturdays.

By virtue of the undisputed tenets of his ancient faith, Braunfeld was obliged to honor the Sabbath and thus could not open his store for business on that faith-mandated day of rest and worship. To require a conscientious Sabbath observer to remain closed on Sundays, however, would prove financially ruinous for him and other observant Jews.

The court, speaking through Chief Justice Warren, turned a deaf ear to Braunfeld's challenge. For reasons of public well-being, the court held the state legislature was within its rights to require a universal day of rest. Since Sunday was the most common day off in American society (once again illustrating how law embodies and reflects mainstream culture) the Pennsylvania legislature had made a perfectly reasonable choice. Nothing more was required, the court held, to pass constitutional muster.

This simple and soothing analysis was, upon reflection, constitutional apostasy. In deep dissent was a relatively new member of the court, William Brennan of New Jersey, who had been appointed by President Eisenhower. Like so many Eisenhower appointees, including Chief Justice Warren, Justice Brennan tilted strongly in favor of individual liberty against the powers of government. And, so it was in the Sunday closing case.

In a masterstroke, Justice Brennan's written dissent maintained that the court's anti-liberty approach upholding the Sunday closing laws created unnecessary tension with its already-settled approach toward cases involving freedom of speech. In free-speech cases, Justice Brennan reminded his colleagues, the court insisted on a rigorous, searching analysis called "strict scrutiny." In his view, the same standard should apply to cases involving the exercise of religious belief.

But what did he mean by "strict scrutiny?" Put simply, if a law or regulation was challenged on the basis of freedom of speech, the court required the government to prove a "compelling" interest justifying the law. Then, and even harder, the government had to demonstrate that it had regulated or legislated in the least liberty-intrusive way.

It was (and remains to this day) a tough test, and Justice Brennan knew as much. In fact, in most free-speech cases, the government is unable to clear the "strict scrutiny" hurdle. If applied as Justice Brennan argued the test should be, the Sunday closing laws would certainly not pass constitutional muster.

The rationale that was unable to carry the day in the Sunday closing cases won favor only a few short years later in Adell Sherbert's employment benefits case. The justices reflected, and with deepened insight changed their minds. It was the same process that we saw in the flag-salute case. Upon further reflection, the court went in a different direction.

Most importantly for the court, and entirely without explanation, Chief Justice Warren flipped. In silence, he simply joined Justice Brennan's opinion upholding Adell Sherbert's claim for benefits. Just like that, almost overnight, the court's approach to free-exercise cases became realigned, consistent with that of free-speech cases. The mighty, pro-freedom approach of "strict scrutiny" would be applied to all cases involving the free exercise of religion.

In contrast to Abraham Braunfeld's attempt to remain open on Sundays, Adell Sherbert prevailed in her quest to remain true to her faith. Under the Supreme Court's newly applied "strict scrutiny" standard, South Carolina failed to show why it could not create an exception permitting Ms. Sherbert to receive her unemployment benefits, thereby permitting her to honor the tenets of her Sabbatarian faith.

Sherbert v. Verner proved to be a game changer for friends of freedom. With the stroke of a pen, the court granted religious liberty the same dignity and power already given to freedom of speech. In that way, *Sherbert* was a transformational case, one that echoed down the corridors of time and into the halls of Congress (as we shall see in a later chapter). Not to give spoilers, but the *Sherbert* decision was showcased by an almost unanimous Congress in enacting the Religious Freedom Restoration Act of 1993.

THE RELIGIOUS RIGHT TO HOME SCHOOLING

Sherbert v. Verner was a monumental case, but it does not stand alone.

Though it may be one of the most important cases in the religious freedom Hall of Fame, it's joined by another case: the Amish religious liberty case, *Wisconsin v. Yoder*.

Chief Justice Warren had by then retired, replaced by Richard Nixon's appointee, Chief Justice Warren Burger. Hailing from Minnesota, and with an inspiring American success story of triumphing over early challenges (including childhood polio), Chief Justice Burger brought a Midwesterner's common sense to bear in his jurisprudence. Theory and doctrine were less important than practicality, as illustrated by his opinion for an almost-unanimous court in the transformational case of *Wisconsin v. Yoder*, a case involving what we would now call a form of "homeschooling."

The Amish community in Wisconsin sought assiduously to maintain the simplicity of their historic lifestyle and culture. They believed children should leave the public-school system upon completion of the eighth grade. By that time, as the Amish saw it, children would have mastered basic academic skills, the "three Rs" in particular, and would be able to function effectively and productively in life. The Amish held that once their children reached high school, regardless of age, they should be sheltered in their own religious community rather than be exposed to the countercultural influences and secular pedagogy they would inevitably face in the public-school system.

The Amish belief came into conflict with the demands of a Wisconsin state law requiring students to remain in school until they reached their sixteenth birthday. Like the *Barnette* case, it was yet another state attempt to coerce students and their families to lay down their religious beliefs and practices. The government, in effect, was overruling the Amish's religious convictions about child rearing.

Once again, state law was clashing with the free exercise of religious faith and freedom of conscience.

In contrast to the values of fervent patriotism undergirding West Virginia's compulsory flag salute ceremony at issue in the *Barnette* case, Wisconsin championed more fundamental interests in fashioning its compulsory education laws. In the policymakers' view, education until a specific age had been reached was vitally important to success in life and in active, engaged citizenship.

No one could reasonably doubt the "compelling" nature of Wisconsin's interest in assuring that its students were adequately educated. A line had to be drawn, just as lines had been drawn for the legal drinking age or the age to vote. A schoolchild's sixteenth birthday seemed a sensible demarcation.

The Supreme Court, speaking through Chief Justice Burger, readily conceded the point. Still, for reasons that lie enshrouded in internal Supreme Court history, Chief Justice Burger chose not to use the pivotal term of art, "strict scrutiny." Though that was the agreed-upon approach to First Amendment analysis, which now included free exercise, Chief Justice Burger suggested a "balancing" process was appropriate and compared the Amish community's interests with those of state government.

It was discretion-filled language, language that causes great discomfort among textualists, most prominently in recent times Justices Clarence Thomas and the late Antonin Scalia (who died in my native Texas in 2017). After all, doesn't "balancing" sound as if judges have all the power to weigh competing interests and come to their own judgment as to which side has the weightier case? Wouldn't that allow for judicial activism when it comes to matters between the government and individual citizens? Wouldn't it allow judges to all but create law in their interpretation?

That sounds a lot like what legislators do.

Sticking with the already-settled standard of "strict scrutiny," in contrast, helps avoid doctrinal squabbles and enhances predictability, a major goal of the judicial process. Yet, a close reading of the chief justice's opinion leaves little doubt that in speaking for the court, he was in fact applying the well-established (and demanding) standard of "strict scrutiny." (Why Chief Justice Burger didn't simply invoke the standard by name, I'll likely never know.)

Fairly read, however, Chief Justice Burger's opinion demonstrates a keen awareness of the great strength of the government's interest in compulsory education. Still, the Chief indicates that this exceedingly strong interest must yield to the Amish community's profound interest in preserving their religious way of life in an increasingly secularized culture.

In other words, if the government wanted to make Amish children continue in school, they'd have to come up with a much more compelling reason.

But, how did he reach this conclusion?

Chief Justice Burger looked to the long and rich history of the Amish religious movement "beginning with the Swiss Anabaptists of the sixteenth century who rejected institutionalized churches and sought to return to the early, simple, Christian life de-emphasizing material success, rejecting the competitive spirit, and seeking to insulate themselves from the world."[10] He quoted from Paul's epistle to the Romans: "Be not conformed to this world," and wrote sympathetically of the Amish response to the Pauline injunction: "This command is fundamental to the Amish faith."[11]

Allowing the state to intrude into the educational and spiritual principles animating the Amish community, he intimated, would be to risk its erosion or even its destruction as a way of life. That, or it would force the Amish to move elsewhere to find a more tolerant and accepting polity. The latter scenario would be a terrible consequence. After all, "forced migration of religious minorities was an evil that lay at the heart of the Religion Clauses [of the First Amendment]."[12]

It wasn't a unanimous opinion, but the Amish won in a landslide. The only dissenting voice was that of Justice William O. Douglas, who, like Justice Jackson, was an appointee of President Franklin Roosevelt. The idiosyncratic justice from Yakima, WA, was predictably progressive throughout his long service on the nation's highest court. In fact, his extrajudicial writing, particularly a provocative polemic entitled "Points of Rebellion," sparked vehement criticism by virtue of its radical call for revolution. The bestselling tome moved then-House Minority Leader (and future president) Gerald Ford to introduce a resolution in the House of Representatives calling for the justice's impeachment.

But in the Amish case, even the colorful Justice Douglas didn't defer entirely to the state. In his partial dissent, he deferred to the court's judgment, iterating that parents had long held the right to educate their own children. That, of course, means what we now know as "homeschooling."

Justice Douglas's narrow but important concern, and thus the reason for his partial dissent, was focused on the trial record compiled in the Wisconsin trial court. In the progressive justice's view, the trial record was unclear that to remain in the Amish community was actually the sincere desire of all the schoolchildren involved in the case. Justice Douglas wanted the state court to hear from all the children, not just some of them, as representatives of the broader Amish community:

> On this important and vital matter of education, I think the children should be entitled to be heard. [...] [The child] may want to be a pianist, or an astronaut, or an oceanographer.[13]

Importantly, however, the dissenting justice was willing to accede to the children's views, such as those of Freda Yoder, a teenager who testified that she truly wanted to remain in her community.

Wisconsin v. Yoder demonstrates the force of religious liberty claims even in the face of an indisputably powerful state interest, that of compulsory education of the young. What's more, and to reiterate a very important practical point for the current era, the case pointed the way for the eventual vindication of homeschooling programs.

In a specific way, then, the *Yoder* case transcends the *Barnette* case in importance in the pantheon of religious freedom jurisprudence. The reason? It demonstrates the special status enjoyed by religious-based perspectives in our constitutional order. To that point, the following language of the court merits careful reflection:

> A way of life, however virtuous and admirable, may not be interposed as a reasonable barrier to reasonable state regulation of education if it is based on purely secular considerations; to have the protection of the Religion Clauses, the claims must be rooted in a religious belief.[14]

This intriguing passage is most important, and it remains the law of the land. Religion is not just special; it is of extraordinary constitutional importance.

As with freedom of speech and the press, it is identified specifically in the First Amendment as worthy of protection.

Thanks to this ruling, Freda Yoder and her fellow Amish students were able to leave school to remain an integral part of their separationist faith community. It was her constitutional right. As a result, she did not get caught up in the swirling debate that forms the basis of examination for our next chapter: prayer in the public schools.

— 4 —

CONSTITUTIONAL COMBAT ZONE

The Battle Over School Prayer

"Ken, they're just trying to take one more valuable thing away from us."

Preparing for an upcoming Supreme Court argument, I was on the phone with Judge Griffin Bell, a former federal appellate judge and Attorney General of the United States under President Jimmy Carter. He was very special to me, and I was eager for his wisdom. Having served as a law clerk for his colleague and contemporary, Judge David Dyer of Miami of the United States Court of Appeals for the Fifth Circuit, I saw firsthand what a wise and honest judge the former Attorney General was. What was the pressing topic *du jour*? The Constitution of the United States.

I was seeking counsel from the learned judge on an upcoming argument in the case of *Lee v. Weisman*, a case pending before the Supreme Court. The issue: school prayer, specifically, graduation prayer. Since I was then serving as the Solicitor General under President George H.W. Bush, our office had already filed an *amicus curiae* brief, a brief submitted as a "friend of the court" arguing in favor of ceremonial school prayer.

Now, I was preparing for the oral argument. Judge Bell had followed the issue and he knew the facts of the case well. Still, he asked what arguments we'd raised.

Before launching into the arguments, I recited the facts.

Consistent with custom and tradition in the Pawtucket, RI, public-school system, Principal Robert E. Lee of Nathan Bishop Middle School had invited Rabbi Leslie Gutterman of Temple Beth-El to offer an invocation and benediction at the school's graduation ceremony. In preparation for the ceremony, Principal Lee had furnished Rabbi Gutterman with a pamphlet setting forth guidelines for both Christian and Jewish clergy. There was no compulsion contained in the pamphlet, only just guidance. What's more, there was no pre-ceremony review by school officials of what the rabbi intended to say in his prayers. Under Pawtucket's tradition-honoring practice, the clergyperson could pray as he or she saw fit.

Prior to the graduation ceremony, Daniel Weisman, whose daughter was among those attending the ceremony, sought a temporary restraining order to stop Rabbi Gutterman from offering the prayer. Weisman's challenge failed, and the show went on as planned.

At the graduation ceremony, the rabbi offered two beautiful prayers, both drawn entirely from the Hebrew scriptures. Though this could have been the end of the issue, it wasn't.

After the ceremony, Mr. Weisman again filed for relief, requesting the court to permanently enjoin the school system from inviting clergy to offer prayers at school ceremonies. The district court agreed with Mr. Weisman, finding the practice violated the establishment clause. The court entered a permanent injunction, effectively putting a halt to the school's long-standing tradition. On appeal, the United States Court of Appeals for the First Circuit affirmed the decision, setting up a Supreme Court challenge.

I had carefully reviewed the case and thought the facts were made in heaven. The noble and limited purpose of the prayer guidelines issued by the school was to suggest safe harbors to avoid understandable concerns that a particular faith community might find itself denigrated or marginalized by a particularly insensitive prayer. What's more, the pamphlet advised Rabbi Gutterman that the prayer should be non-sectarian. It seemed to me that the practice and pamphlet provided plenty of assurance of constitutionality.

The litigation was not directed personally at Rabbi Gutterman or his specific prayers, drawn as they were from ancient scripture. Rather, Mr. Weisman was attacking the entire custom of clergy-delivered graduation prayers, which, in my view and the view of my colleagues at the Solicitor General's office, seemed like an overreach.

No one was compelled to attend the graduation, and couldn't they simply step out during the prayers or just ignore them by concentrating on the graduation program that had been handed out? The establishment clause surely couldn't be used to strike down such a time-honored, nonsectarian, noncoercive ceremonial practice, particularly in light of the long and established history of legislative prayer. Surely, we thought, the practice was consistent with the Supreme Court's rulings in *Barnette* and *Wisconsin v. Yoder*; that is, since there was no coercion, it followed that there was nothing unconstitutional in the practice. Right?

Wrong, Judge Bell worried.

A loyal Democrat appointed by President Kennedy, and an unabashed admirer of hallowed traditions, Judge Bell feared the worst. The court might well strike down this long-established practice. Though he couldn't pinpoint exactly why, this kind of ceremonial prayer had a different "feel" than legislative prayer, he thought. This was, after all, prayer in the context of a public school.

Turns out, Judge Bell's worries were well founded.

On behalf of the George H.W. Bush administration, I argued the case before the Supreme Court, and after months of waiting for a decision, we received the stunning news: we didn't just lose, but our very rationale for justifying graduation prayers was turned ju-jitsu-like against us.

Speaking through Justice Anthony Kennedy, a Reagan appointee and a pivotally important "swing vote" member of the court for many years, the school's traditional practice was struck down. As Justice Kennedy and the court majority saw it, a graduation ceremony was, for all intents and purposes, mandatory. It represented the culmination of an important academic journey and thus had deep meaning for the graduates and their families.

So, as a practical matter (as opposed to a matter of law as in *Barnette* and *Yoder*), graduates and their loved ones were obliged to be present. In the majority's view, government compulsion or coercion (those evils identified so powerfully by Justice Jackson's opinion in *Barnette*) was present in the graduation context.

Not only that, the majority found that Nathan Bishop's principal had constitutionally erred. By providing prayer guidelines, even though trying to be sensitive to the audience's feelings, the government was guiding and shaping Rabbi Gutterman's prayers. Thus, it had inadvertently stepped across the constitutional line into territory forbidden by the establishment clause.

No lawyer likes to lose a case, but this loss was especially bitter. What we viewed as our strengths—a venerable American public-school tradition with no feature of mandatory attendance, coupled with thoughtful, non-divisive prayers offered by a minority-faith clergyman—turned out ironically to be fatal weaknesses.

Why?

The court's majority shrugged off our arguments of noncoercion as wooden formalism. The justices in the majority believed there was an informal but very real pressure for a graduating student and her family to be physically present at such a signal event, a milestone in life's journey. Though I'd chosen to forgo my own graduation ceremony in the past (I'd missed my law school commencement, for instance) the court's argument rang as intellectually honest, even though I profoundly disagreed.

My colleagues and I also failed to apprehend just how the court would view the school district's practice of guiding the clergymen in framing their respective prayers. Again, as with the factor of attendance itself, the official guidance provided by the school district was not mandatory, and the clergy could have ignored it entirely and prayed in keeping with their faith tradition. Still, the official effort to guide and shape the prayers tied the seemingly innocuous process to the school prayer cases that had rocked the nation during the Warren court era. It was a strange connection, bordering on a contrivance. The Nathan Bishop graduation prayers offered by Rabbi Weisman were, by any fair measure, light years away from the swirling controversy that had resulted in calls for the impeachment of Chief Justice Warren.

Let's explore why.

PRAYER IN THE WARREN COURT

In the early 1960s a series of school-prayer cases made their way up to the Supreme Court. In what had long been considered a Christian nation, perhaps even a nation of prayer, the Supreme Court, under Chief Justice Earl Warren, was preparing to shock the country with two opinions on the appropriate role, if any, of prayer in public schools.

In the first of these stunning cases, *Engel v. Vitale*, decided in 1962, the State of New York had indulged in framing an official morning prayer and required its recitation before the start of every school day. (Happily, there was a nod to conscientious objectors, allowing students to refrain from participating.)

The text of the official prayer was as follows: "Almighty God, we acknowledge our dependence upon Thee, and we beg Thy blessings upon us, our parents, our teachers, and our Country."

It was a prayer expressed beautifully in Elizabethan English (likely drawn from the King James Version of the Bible) and there's no doubt Abraham Lincoln and Robert Jackson would have been drawn to the prayer's elegant language.

Notice, also, the simplicity of the prayer. It was a plea, an acknowledgement of dependence on God, and a request for a blessing. It echoed the language of the Preamble to America's Constitution, which speaks of "the Blessings of Liberty." Many Americans, certainly during the fifties and early sixties, would have found the prayer not only inoffensive, but inspiring and noble in sentiment.

It is also important to remember the historical context. The controversy in *Engel v. Vitale* arose during the age of national concern with

"Godless Communism," as practiced in the former Soviet Union and in Communist China. The prayer might have been viewed culturally as a hedge against Communism.

That said, many people professing faith would have seen this eloquent prayer as far from perfect. There was no reference to Jesus Christ and, of course, faithful Catholics would have deemed the official prayer discordantly incomplete with its omission, "In the name of the Father, and of the Son, and of the Holy Spirit."

What's more, the prayer failed to include a simple "Amen" at the conclusion. Though these omissions didn't make any particular sect happy, didn't that indicate just how nonsectarian it was?

Textual quibbles aside, a more fundamental flaw infected New York State's school-prayer ceremony. As inoffensive as the prayer may have been to the vast majority of students and parents, it was fashioned by the State of New York.

This was not a clergyperson, say a school chaplain (a theoretical counterpart to the Nebraska chaplain in *Marsh v. Chambers*, as discussed in Chapter 2) offering a prayer unhindered by school officials (and thus not constituting official governmental action for constitutional purposes). Even more importantly for constitutional purposes, the challenged prayer was not voluntarily led by a student at the beginning of class.

Speaking for a majority of the court, Justice Hugo Black (a President Franklin D. Roosevelt appointee like Justice Robert Jackson) wrote:

> [W]e think that the constitutional prohibition against laws respecting an establishment of religion must at least mean that in this country it is no part of the business of government to compose official prayers for any group of the American people to recite as a part of a religious program carried on by government.[1]

Pretty straightforward, and few would argue with that rationale.

In essence, the court concluded that composing prayers for recitation in the public schools, or in any other official activity, constituted government overreach. To allow this practice would run afoul of the non-establishment requirement restraining all governmental action at federal, state, and local levels.

True, the Empire State's law contemplated an exception for conscientious objectors. Students could opt out. The lesson of *West Virginia Board of Education v. Barnette* (which we discussed in Chapter 3) did not go unheeded by the educators. But an opt-out provision, thoughtful though it was, could not wash away the original sin of the government fashioning and framing prayers.

Truth be told, the overwhelming majority of believers who take the time to analyze carefully the Warren court's basic holding would likely agree with it.

Over the ensuing years, the opinion in this case has been wildly overread. The court did not ban prayer in public schools under any and all circumstances. Far from it. To the contrary, what was constitutionally offensive was much more limited, namely, the official sponsorship of prayers that aligned the government with an expression of faith.

The court's ruling was limited. It created a clear distinction. What a state could do in certain free-speech contexts, it could not do with religious speech. Though a state or local government could lawfully require the recitation of a state-crafted pledge (subject to conscientious objectors' protections), it could not require the recitation of a state-crafted prayer.

With that distinction in mind, we return to the New York State prayer itself. The text ineluctably suggests that the state school board was seeking to inculcate moral and spiritual values within the Empire State's student population. The words are those of a broad "civic religion," similar to the placement of the words "under God" in the Pledge of Allegiance, or the creation of the national motto "In God we trust." New York State officials doubtlessly hoped to accomplish goals similar to those embraced by the West Virginia educators in *Barnette*, with an added dimension of hoped-for spiritual development. On its face, that's an admirable objective.

Yet, these noble hopes and dreams were misplaced. Justice Black continued in his rationale:

It is a matter of history that this very practice of establishing govern-mentally-composed prayers for religious services was one of the reasons which caused many of our early colonists to leave England and seek religious freedom in America.[2]

The beautifully worded Book of Common Prayer was, Justice Black reminded the nation, a product not just of the officially-established church, but of governmental action in the mother country:

> The Book of Common Prayer, which was created under governmental direction and which was approved by Acts of Parliament in 1548 and 1549, set out in minute detail the accepted form and content of prayer and other religious ceremonies to be used in the established, tax-supported Church of England.[3]

As elegantly crafted as it is, the Book of Common Prayer was by no means universally accepted at the time of its original publication:

> The controversies over the Book and what should be its content repeatedly threatened to disrupt the peace of that country as the accepted forms of prayer in the established church changed with the views of the particular ruler that happened to be in control at that time.[4]

Wise governments strive for unity within the polity. But in matters of faith and belief, achieving uniformity inevitably requires coercion, which in turn leads to strife and unrest, or as America's history shows, to religious dissenters seeking a better life, a life of freedom.

THY KINGDOM COME, BUT NOT BY COERCION

The second school-prayer case likewise shook the nation. At issue was a growing practice in state educational systems of requiring daily recitation of scripture and the Lord's Prayer. In 1963, it all came to a head in Pennsylvania in the case of *Abington School District v. Schempp*.

Consistent with a statewide law, public school days in the Commonwealth were to begin with a Bible reading. Particularly, a state statute required that:

> At least ten verses from the Holy Bible shall be read, without comment, at the opening of each public school on each school day. Any child shall be excused from such Bible reading, or attending such Bible reading, upon the written request of his parent or guardian.[5]

In Abington Township, and in many districts around the state, the Bible reading was followed by the Lord's Prayer.[6] What's more, though the student reading the Bible verse could select another translation, the school only provided the King James Version of the Bible for the morning readings.

Not every family in the Keystone State was pleased with the legislation. In fact, the Schempp family brought suit to enjoin enforcement of the law, contending the practice violated their constitutional rights.

The Pennsylvania case featured a full trial in state court, which was highly revealing. Expert witnesses testified as to the inevitable divisiveness of reading from one version or another of the Bible. Not all communities of faith accepted the King James Version. Moreover, experts testified that portions of the New Testament were offensive to the Jewish tradition.

Unlike the case in New York, no state-crafted prayer was recited. Nonetheless, the state government was actively siding with a particular religious perspective, especially with the officially-sanctioned recitation of the Lord's Prayer. Consistent with *Barnette*, the state provided an exit ramp—the student could leave the classroom during the opening scripture reading and prayer. Still, was that enough?

The testimony of Edward Schempp, father of two of the children who challenged Pennsylvania's practice, was especially poignant. As faithful Unitarians, the Schempp family took exception to many biblical doctrines, and the children specifically noted that "all of the doctrines to which they referred were read to them at various times as part of the exercise."[7]

At the conclusion of the trial, the court struck down the Pennsylvania statute. The trial court found:

> The reading of the verses, even without comment, possesses a devotional and religious character and constitutes, in effect, a religious observance. The devotional and religious nature of the morning exercises is made all the more apparent by the fact that the Bible reading is followed immediately by a recital in unison by the pupils of the Lord's Prayer. The fact that some pupils, or, theoretically, all pupils, might be excused from attendance at the exercises does not mitigate the obligatory nature of the ceremony, for [the statute] unequivocally requires the exercises to be held every school day in every school in the Commonwealth. The exercises are held in the school buildings, and perforce are conducted by and under the authority of the local school authorities, and during school sessions. Since the statute requires the reading of the 'Holy Bible,' a Christian document, the practice [...] prefers the Christian religion. The record demonstrates that it was the intention of [...] the Commonwealth [...] to introduce a religious ceremony into the public schools of the Commonwealth.[8]

The case was appealed all the way to the Supreme Court. There, Justice Tom Clark (a Texan appointee of President Truman) wrote the majority opinion, noting two fundamental problems with the seemingly harmless, even benign, practice promoted by the Commonwealth of Pennsylvania. First, the state government was officially aligning itself with one faith perspective, namely Protestant Christianity. As mentioned earlier, the state authorities provided the King James Version of the Bible to the thousands of classrooms around the Commonwealth, which included New Testament passages. Catholic parents would naturally be concerned about this exclusivity of biblical perspective (they preferred the Douay version of the Bible), as would Jewish believers, who would obviously not embrace the idea of readings from the New Testament.

Second, objecting schoolchildren would inevitably feel coerced, or at least their parents would understandably worry about their children's relationships with both their teachers and their fellow classmates. The students would be setting themselves apart from the majority, a daunting thing to ask of young schoolchildren. In fact, Justice Clark seemed to imply that coercion could take different shapes. He wrote, "[Mr. Schempp] testified that if [his two children] were excused from Bible reading they would have to stand in the hall outside their 'homeroom' and that this carried with it the imputation of punishment for bad conduct."[9]

The Pennsylvania statute violated the establishment clause. So ruled the Supreme Court by a stunning 8-1 margin.

THE IRONY OF PRAYER

Fierce reaction erupted condemning both *Engel v. Vitale* and *Abington School District v. Schempp*. The Warren court was widely excoriated for its perceived hostility to religion. Ironically, though, in both school-prayer cases, the court emphasized America's history and tradition of religious liberty. In fact, in *Engel v. Vitale*, Justice Black, another largely self-taught member of the court, wrote:

> By the time of the adoption of the Constitution, our history shows that [the people] knew, some of them from bitter personal experience, that one of the greatest dangers to the freedom of the individual to worship in his own way lay in the Government's placing its official stamp of approval upon one particular kind of prayer or one particular form of religious services. They knew the anguish, hardship, and bitter strife that could come when religious groups struggled with one another to obtain the Government's stamp of approval from each King, Queen, or Protector that came to temporary power.[10]

Avoidance of strife within the country was one of the animating purposes of the religion clauses, a concern reflected in the Bladensburg Cross case decades later.

But it wasn't just Justice Black who held this concern. Justice William O. Douglas captured the thought in this passage (in his separate opinion in *Engel v. Vitale*): "[O]nce government finances a religious exercise [such as the mandatory reading of Bible verses] it inserts a divisive influence into our communities."[11]

Ironically, the Warren court's concern about avoiding religious-related strife was overwhelmed by the acrimony flowing in the wake of the justices' landmark decisions. In trying to avoid division, the justices had unwittingly spawned bitter division.

Thirty years later, in the graduation prayer case, *Lee v. Weisman*, that division continued. Could a happy middle ground be found?

As we will see, it could, and it would come in the form of returning to the Great Principles. It would come in allowing students to exercise their religious rights independently, apart from intrusion by government officials. After all, this is the very object the First Amendment was meant to protect: individual liberty, even of the youngest believers.

America's first freedom was not meant to unleash government officials, no matter how well-meaning, to mandate religious observances and frame "official" prayers.

— 5 —

DISCRIMINATION IN
THE SCHOOLHOUSE

S itting in judgment on the constitutionality of a government action
is one of the weightiest duties of the Supreme Court, especially
when the alleged violation is an act of Congress.

In turn, defending acts of Congress whose constitutionality is under
scrutiny by the Supreme Court is one of the most humbling duties of
the Solicitor General, as a senior officer of the Department of Justice.
Since the Solicitor General is part of the Executive Branch, the stakes
in these cases are always high, especially when all three branches of
the federal government square off in a constitutional clash.

During my own service as Solicitor General under President George
H.W. Bush, I was involved in one such clash thanks to Bridget Mergens
and her brave battle for religious liberty. The issue raised by Mergens
was fundamental in a free society: whether her school district violated
the Equal Access Act of 1984 by refusing to allow her to organize an
after-school Bible study on her school campus. The corollary issue?
Was the Equal Access Act constitutional or, instead, did it violate the
establishment clause?

As its name suggests, the Equal Access Act of 1984 sought to
advance the goal of equality in public-school systems that received
federal funds. The concept behind the act was straightforward. If a
secondary school received any federal funds, and the school allowed

one or more student-led extracurricular groups to meet on campus, then the school was obliged to provide "equal access" to all extracurricular groups, including religious groups.

The only caveat was that there could be no disruption of the educational process.

The law was challenged by a woefully misguided public-school system in suburban Omaha, NE. The school claimed that the act violated the establishment clause to the extent it required public schools to permit religious clubs to operate on campus.

But what were the facts giving rise to the dispute?

The case came in the wake of the raging school-prayer controversy of the 1960s and '70s, as we discussed in the prior chapter. Badly misreading the school-prayer cases, numerous school districts blocked the efforts of students to engage in religious activity on their own secondary school campuses.

Bridget Mergens was one such student, a casualty of overzealous school authorities seeking to exclude entirely voluntary religious activity led by Mergens and her friends. Believing the Equal Access Act unconstitutional, those misguided local school authorities flagrantly violated the act and the principles of equality contained within it. And so, the courts needed to step in.

MERGENS AND THE FIGHT FOR EQUALITY

Consider the facts of Bridget Mergens's case. As a high-school sophomore, Bridget entered Westside High School in suburban Omaha, with a Spirit-filled goal. A devout evangelical Christian, she was eager to launch an extracurricular group, namely a Bible study club that would be open to all students, not just to Christian believers. For Bridget, holding up a welcome sign, figuratively speaking, was both important and at the very heart of what she wanted the club to be; namely, a safe place for one and all.

The school authorities were not so welcoming, however. They rejected her request, recommending she and her group meet at a nearby church. That was the appropriate venue for a student religious group, the authorities urged. Bridget's response was polite but firm: the church down the street wasn't her home church. She and her like-minded classmates had the right to meet on school grounds, just like the thirty (or more) extracurricular groups that regularly met on campus after the school day ended. If the French Club, the Chess Club, and even the Dungeons and Dragons Club (among many others) could organize and hold regular meetings on campus so, too, could her Bible study group. The law, after all, granted them equal access to school grounds.

This raises an important point, constitutionally speaking. Bridget Mergens was not asking for preferential treatment. She was no Joseph, asking for favored treatment and the many-colored coat that came with it, from Jacob. And remember Mrs. Sherbert, the devout Seventh Day Adventist (discussed in Chapter 3), who received unemployment benefits since she couldn't in good conscience work on Saturdays? Adell received a sort of special treatment based on religious belief and practice. So why couldn't Mergens at least receive equal treatment?

Despite her polite insistence upon equal treatment, the school authorities continued to say no. Allowing a Bible study club to meet, they fretted, would run afoul of principles of separation of church and state.

But Mergens would not take no for an answer. After her ensuing appeal to the school board proved unavailing, she exercised the only option she had left. She took the school to court.

Mergens's legal position had two key elements. The first was that singling out her group for discriminatory treatment violated the equality principle embodied in our Constitution, including the Fifth Amendment's due process clause. That clause, as interpreted by the Supreme Court, incorporates the core liberties, which include religious liberty, as rights all Americans enjoy for protection against actions by their state and local governments. Happily, the constitutional demand for equality was expressly laid out in the Fourteenth Amendment, ratified in the wake of the Civil War.

The second prong of her challenge invoked the Equal Access Act of 1984, passed overwhelmingly by Congress and signed into law by President Reagan. The measure was designed to prevent exactly what the Westside School Board was doing—discriminating against religious clubs that wanted to meet on campus. Just as with Westside High School, school authorities around the country permitted a wide range of extracurricular student organizations to meet, but all too frequently said no to religious clubs.

This was blatant, purposeful discrimination.

In an 8-1 decision, the Supreme Court upheld the Equal Access Act, and thus Mergens's right to convene the club on campus. Although a lopsided majority agreed on the bottom line (Bridget Mergens wins), a variety of separate opinions were issued.

Justice Thurgood Marshall (the first African-American jurist to serve on the Supreme Court) supported the majority opinion, but wrote separately. He demanded that school authorities make clear that Westside was not endorsing the Christian club's views.

But speaking through Justice Sandra Day O'Connor (the first female jurist to serve on the Supreme Court) the majority firmly rejected Justice Marshall's asserted demands on the school system. There was safety in numbers, the majority said. The thirty or so student clubs meeting on the Westside campus made it crystal clear that this extracurricular potpourri was the result of students' myriad interests, a grassroots explosion of wide-ranging organizations, not the result of a dictate from the principal's office. As Justice O'Connor put it, "To the extent that a religious club is merely one of many different student-initiated clubs, students should perceive no message of government endorsement of religion."[1]

Not all members of the majority were as concerned with "endorsement," even in schools where fewer clubs convened. In particular, Justice Kennedy, joined by Justice Scalia, emphasized in a separate opinion that two elements of the Equal Access Act satisfied the constitutional command of non-establishment. First, the statute did not contemplate schools providing direct aid, such as financial support, to religious clubs, and therefore, there was no "establishment" of religion. Second, nothing in the statute pointed to or authorized the herding of students into Christian clubs or prayer groups; in other words, there were no indicators of coercion. They fretted that the term "endorsement," embraced by Justice O'Connor and insisted upon by Justice Marshall, was too ambiguous to serve the important but limited purposes undergirding the establishment clause.

To Justices Kennedy and Scalia, the key characteristic was equality of treatment. In terms of the statute's constitutionality, the characteristic of "no favoritism" toward religious clubs carried the day.

The Equal Access Act was completely upheld. The court sustained federal legislative power to regulate local school authorities receiving federal funds and to prohibit them from discriminating against religious perspectives.

The court's decision in Bridget Mergens's case not only upheld a pro-equality measure passed by Congress, it strengthened the Great Principle of equality that had been tested early in the Reagan administration.

EQUALITY—A CONSTITUTIONAL GOLDEN RULE

The equality issue faced by Mergens first arose in a college setting in the case of *Widmar v. Vincent*. Specifically, administrators at the University of Missouri at Kansas City (UMKC) refused to permit a Christian student group called Petros to meet on the university campus. Again, this represented a blatantly discriminatory policy, one guided by the university's view that allowing the group to meet would violate the establishment clause.

Viewing the case through the lens of freedom of speech protected by the First Amendment, the Supreme Court overwhelmingly sided with the student group. Since the activities that the UMKC group sought to engage in were Christian worship, prayer, singing hymns, and Bible study, the court concluded that their meetings were a form of constitutionally-protected speech, and the university, as a state actor, could not lightly infringe upon that right.

Widmar v. Vincent was decided in 1981, a few years before the ratification of the Equal Access Act. Still, the ruling was consistent with a long line of cases in which the court had expansively interpreted the pivotal term "speech," to include a wide variety of communication, such as music, art, theater and the like. For example, the controversial 1970s musical *Hair*, featuring flashes of countercultural nudity, was deemed by the high court as meriting constitutional protection. Especially relevant to the schoolhouse setting, in a case emerging from Des Moines, IA, in the 1960s, a high schooler was found to have engaged in "symbolic speech" when he wore an armband in class to protest against the Vietnam War.[2]

In contrast to Bridget Mergens's case though, the UMKC case involved college students. Perhaps this is why Mergens's school administrators believed the case did not apply. Perhaps they believed themselves to have a vested interest in protecting secondary school students, who were (presumably) less mature and more impressionable than young adults, from religious encroachment.

This paternalistic concern was seen in the school district's argument. Their stated concern? Creating a "symbolic link" between government and religion, which could lead younger students to the view that "the powers of government" were being employed to support religious activity.

When read together, however, *Widmar v. Vincent*, Congress's passage of the Equal Access Act, and the *Mergens* case all demonstrate the power of the equality principle.

Indeed, the concept of equality has become a sort of constitutional golden rule. Over the years, it's proven to be a powerful weapon in the arsenal of religious liberty's forces. Importantly, it promises to remain so in the years to come.

TAKING THE FIGHT TO THE SCHOOLS

A personal experience brings the point home. Not long after the *Mergens* decision was handed down, I found myself as a banquet speaker at the annual gathering of the Christian Legal Society (on whose board I am now blessed to serve). My remarks focused on the equality principle in general, and the *Mergens* decision in particular. Having argued the case in the Supreme Court, I was in a decent position to respond to a question from one of the attendees.

At the banquet, a gentleman from the crowd spoke up. "General Starr, I appreciated your remarks," he said, "but I have a recent experience in Renton, WA, where I live. The school board there just rejected the request of a Christian club to meet on the high school campus. What should we do?"

My response was simple. The school board was knowingly and intentionally violating the students' rights. That violation was clear under both the United States Constitution and the Equal Access Act. Therefore, they must immediately cease and desist. Then, with all the seriousness I could muster, I asked him to inform the board members that if they didn't change their position, they could be subjected to personal liability for the willful violation of clearly established individual rights, which would trigger potential liability for punitive damages which the taxpayers could not indemnify or reimburse.

Not long afterwards, in those pre-email days, I received a letter from the gentleman. The pro-equality argument had worked. The students' application had just been approved, without dissent.

Equality, and the Equal Access Act, carried the day thanks to the courage and persistence of Bridget Mergens. And this, friends of liberty, is why it pays to understand the constitutional framework of religious freedom.

EQUAL ACCESS BEYOND THE CLASSROOM

The issue of equality and equal access does not simply apply to student prayer groups in public school, however. Consider yet another context where the issue of equality arises, this one drawn from the issue of church access to public property.

In one of his last opinions for the court, Justice Byron White delivered a powerful pro-equality valedictory statement before his retirement during the first year of the Clinton administration. The case, *Lamb's Chapel v. Center Moriches Union Free School District*, emerged in the now-familiar setting: government officials seeking to exclude religious groups from carrying on activities on public property.

The facts could not be more straightforward. Lamb's Chapel, an evangelical church on Long Island, applied to the local school district to get access to school facilities after school hours in order to show a James Dobson film series, divided into six parts, entitled *Turn Your Heart Toward Home*. The series would be open to the public, which would be encouraged to attend.

As with the Westside School District in Omaha and the UMKC authorities in Missouri, the Long Island school district said no. "This film," the district officials responded, "does appear to be church-related and therefore your request must be refused."[3]

This was yet again an example of the baleful pattern of legally-mandated discrimination, not simply the *ad hoc* (if misguided) judgment of school district authorities.

The Empire State had drifted a long way toward enforced secularism since the Supreme Court's decision a generation earlier in the school-prayer cases that stunned the nation. In contrast to that earlier time, New York statutes authorized local school boards to permit school facilities to be used for ten specified purposes, none of which were religious. Among the permitted uses, however, was a broadly-worded authorization that would, by its terms, readily include Lamb's Chapel's application. Specifically, the school district could appropriately permit "social, civic, and recreational meetings and entertainments, and other uses pertaining to the welfare of the community."

James Dobson's film series fitted squarely within the heartland of the catch-all clause.

How?

The first of the six-part series was entitled: "A Father Looks Back." According to a pamphlet submitted to the school authorities, that inaugural segment "emphasizes how swiftly time passes and appeals to all parents to 'turn their hearts toward home' during the all-important child-rearing years."[4] Each of the six segments dealt with important family questions, including a video entitled "Overcoming a Painful Childhood."

Surely this was a positive, pro-community-welfare series. But as befits a James Dobson series, the perspective undergirding the film was unapologetically Christian in nature, a dimension that sounded the death knell for its public screening under New York's separationist law.

The lower courts once again got it wrong, sustaining the school officials' "faith communities need not apply" approach. Once again, the Supreme Court, this time unanimous in its judgment, slapped down the lower courts for their anti-liberty decisions.

The neighboring clause in the First Amendment, the free-speech clause, was summoned onto the battlefield and proved the decisive volley in support of freedom. Firmly embedded in that clause, the court said, was the "equality" or "non-discrimination" principle. A school, the court stated, could not single out and discriminate against certain kinds of speech on school property. If anyone was allowed access to speak freely, all should be allowed the same access.

Writing for the majority, Justice White agreed that school authorities should be allowed to preserve school property for limited, specified uses. If the circus came to town, it shouldn't be able to demand access to school grounds on the theory that the United Way or the local Lions' Club was granted access. Indeed, school authorities could properly declare, "these facilities are closed, period, save for educating the district's children during school hours."

But that's not what New York's law contemplated, nor what the school authorities on Long Island actually did. The schoolhouse doors were warmly opened for after-school hours usage by community groups, but they weren't open to all organizations.

In stark contrast to secular organizations, religious organizations weren't welcome.

Quoting from prior case law, Justice White laid down the equality principle in these words: "The principle that has emerged from our cases 'is that the First Amendment forbids the government to regulate speech in ways that favor some viewpoints or ideas at the expense of others.'"[5]

The court relied heavily on the UMKC case (*Widmar v. Vincent*, as discussed), providing a helpful illustration of how the Supreme Court creates a body of jurisprudence, case by case, year after year.

As the examples in this chapter show, equality provides a powerful organizing principle for friends of freedom. It is a truly Great Principle, ready to be summoned in the pro-freedom fight.

Its application by the Supreme Court has resulted in victory after victory for the cause of religious liberty. Its power has been further enhanced by the fact that Congress and various presidents have rallied to the cause.

With this principle in mind, let's pause. Let's turn from the Supreme Court's pro-freedom labors and focus on two other centers of power in the nation's capital, the White House and Capitol Hill. They, too, can be—and frequently are—friends of liberty.

— 6 —

FRIENDS IN HIGH PLACES

The Oval Office and Capitol Hill

Every year, on the first Thursday in February, the President, leaders of Congress, and various officials from the Executive Branch gather in the cavernous main ballroom of the Washington Hilton. The event was the National Prayer Breakfast. It's attended by thousands of faithful individuals from around the world and gives new meaning to "ecumenical," with numerous communities of faith represented. Tickets are pricey, yet always in short supply.

As is always the case, the February 2020 event was sold out, and it fell just one day after President Trump's acquittal by the deeply-divided Senate in his historic impeachment trial. As is the tradition, President Trump was the keynote speaker. It was sure to be a memorable event.

With Speaker of the House Nancy Pelosi sitting prominently at the head table, the president began his remarks by brandishing a copy of that morning's *Washington Post*. The banner headline read: "Trump Acquitted." And with that, it became evident that the text of the president's speech had not been drawn from the Sermon on the Mount.

My wife Alice and I try to attend every year, so we're no strangers to this event. Although it is ordinarily an inspiring, uplifting gathering, the tone of this sixty-eighth annual gathering was starkly different than any that had come before. (It was even different than those occurring during the stormy days of the Nixon and Clinton administrations.) This one was doomed to be a much more combative affair, an event more representative of the nation's cultural moment.

In less tumultuous times, however, the National Prayer Breakfast has stood as a symbolic display of unity, a happy exception to the political rancor and discord that typically characterizes our political system. It's meant to be a moment where the president, Congress, members of the judiciary, and other leaders from around the country come together under the power of faith, where they lay aside divisive issues and bow a knee to God. In a sense, it's meant to be a metaphor for how our country works best: one nation, under God, indivisible.

As we've seen, the Supreme Court has rallied around critically-important pro-liberty concepts such as freedom of conscience, noncoercion, and equality. Despite the deepening partisan divide between Congress and the president, historically, the Executive and Legislative Branches frequently settle comfortably together into the same political "pew" to defend basic precepts of religious liberty.

The (usual) spirit of the National Prayer Breakfast prevails, time and again, when Capitol Hill and the White House are in dialogue on issues of religious freedom.

We saw that spirit of unity at work in Congress's response to official discrimination directed against secondary-school students when bipartisan majorities in both the House and Senate considered the pro-freedom Equal Access Act. The legislative history of the Equal Access Act demonstrated that Congress was quite upset about two lower-court opinions upholding discriminatory exclusion of faith-focused clubs from public-school campuses, all in the name of honoring the establishment clause.

So, Congress refused to sit idly by and wait for the Supreme Court (hopefully) to cure the constitutional heresy. The result? The act passed by an overwhelming vote and was enthusiastically signed into law by President Ronald Reagan.

It was that bipartisan measure that saved the day for Bridget Mergens' Bible study club.

The story of the Equal Access Act is parable-like, pointing to a larger truth. Time and again, Congress and the president monitor the religious-liberty landscape, step into the fray and strike mighty blows, often collaboratively, in favor of religious freedom.

If I were looking to make my case for this proposition in the court of law, I would call to the stand, so to speak, the most important religious-liberty Congressional reform in the nation's history: the Religious Freedom Restoration Act of 1993.

As with the Equal Access Act, the Religious Freedom Restoration Act, known by its acronym, "RFRA," began as a reaction to judicial decisions. But in contrast to the Equal Access Act, which addressed the lower courts' penchant for discriminating against religion in educational contexts, in RFRA, Congress took aim at a Supreme Court decision written, ironically, by Justice Antonin Scalia, an ordinarily dependable ally in the arena of religious freedom.

What caused Justice Scalia to set his face against religious freedom? We turn now to the story of *Employment Division v. Smith*.

PEYOTE AND THE LIMITS
OF FREE EXPRESSION

In Oregon, the state had passed a sweeping state anti-drug law. The criminal statute forbade the use of various drugs, including peyote, a hallucinogen used in the worship services of the Native American Church. As a result, two members of that faith community, Alfred Smith and Galen Black, were fired from their jobs with a private drug rehabilitation organization. (Consider the irony.)

The reason being that the two church members ingested peyote as part of their Native American worship services. No one doubted the sincerity of their faith, nor the hallowed nature of their church's traditional use of peyote. Still, rules were rules, and the two men found themselves unemployed as a result of their worship practices.

Alfred and Galen applied for unemployment benefits, which were promptly denied by virtue of their discharge on grounds of work-re-lated "misconduct." As the state officials saw it, the two worshipers were at fault.

Smith and Black filed suit, alleging (as had Adell Sherbert a genera-tion earlier) that the state's denial of benefits violated their free exercise rights. This time, in contrast to the South Carolina judges in Adell Sherbert's case, the Oregon courts agreed with the two challengers. The case was appealed and made its way to the judicial pinnacle, where, in a bizarre twist, the divided Supreme Court ruled in favor of the state.

What happened to the religious-freedom protectors at the high court?

Narrowly limiting both *Sherbert v. Verner* (upholding the Seventh Day Adventist's claim for unemployment benefits) and *Wisconsin v. Yoder* (vindicating the Amish community's education approach), the razor-thin 5-4 majority, speaking through Justice Scalia, fashioned an entirely new approach. Now, if a state enforced a law that was generally applicable and "neutral" in terms of religion—that is, if the measure neither favored nor disfavored religion—then the state could go for-ward. In contrast to both *Sherbert* and *Yoder*, however, under Justice Scalia's view, simply by virtue of the free exercise clause, Oregon did not have to carve out a religious-based exception.

Like the school-prayer cases, the Oregon peyote decision came as a shock. This approach had the practical effect of overruling both landmark cases (*Sherbert* and *Yoder*) from the Warren and Burger court eras while officially leaving the two decisions on the books.

Writing for the majority, Justice Scalia tried to skate past *Sherbert* and *Yoder* on rather flimsy grounds.

What were those grounds? Justice Scalia wrote: "The free exercise of religion means, first and foremost, the right to believe and profess whatever religious doctrine one desires. Thus, the First Amendment obviously excluded all 'governmental regulations of beliefs as such.'"[1]

No one in his or her right mind could disagree with that prop-osition. It's hard these days to imagine a government regulation of "beliefs," but on occasion in past decades state governments have strayed into that forbidden territory, such as requiring an oath attesting to one's belief in God. The Supreme Court had unanimously struck down one such attempt by the state of Maryland, which required government officials to take a God-honoring oath.[2]

But, in Justice Scalia's view, actions, as opposed to beliefs, were different. In fact, government regulates actions all the time. The always-creative Justice Scalia conjured up some intriguing examples of actions that might merit a free-exercise-clause-ordained exception: "It would doubtless be unconstitutional, for example, to ban the casting of 'statues that are to be used for worship purposes,' or to prohibit bowing down before a golden calf."[3]

It was a shamefully silly set of examples. Paganism would enjoy protection, as Justice Scalia posited, just as would other faiths. But what state government would seriously contemplate this kind of hypothetical anti-pagan legislation?

These were classic examples of law-school hypotheticals; fruitful thought exercises and fun to discuss, but entirely unrealistic in terms of the way the actual world works.

Shockingly, Justice Scalia invoked an opinion (written by Justice Felix Frankfurter, another appointee of Franklin Roosevelt's) in the long-ago Pennsylvania flag-salute case, *Minersville School District v. Gobitis*. As we saw in Chapter 3, that case had been overruled by the court's groundbreaking decision three years later in *Barnette*.

This was truly beyond the pale. Relying on an overruled case? That's a bit odd, leading with the judicial chin. What's more, Justice Frankfurter's pro-government-power opinion in the Pennsylvania case allowed the societal interest in patriotic conformity to trump the individual's freedom of conscience, which is a notion flatly inconsistent with our basic constitutional values, as made clear in the West Virginia case (*Barnette*).

Unsurprisingly, Justice Scalia's clever opinion drew sharp dissents. Even one of his colleagues who agreed with his bottom line (a practice called "concurring in the judgment") totally disagreed with his freedom-robbing analysis.

As Justice Sandra Day O'Connor saw the case, Oregon had to run the demanding constitutional gauntlet of satisfying "strict scrutiny," the most rigorous standard for testing a statute's constitutionality. In light of the scourge of drugs, including the dangers posed by the hallucinogen peyote, Justice O'Connor approved the Oregon statute as one of those rare birds that could fly successfully through the "strict scrutiny" skies.

The three dissenters, Justices Blackmun, Brennan, and Marshall, castigated the majority for "mischaracterizing the court's precedents," "discard[ing] leading free exercise cases," and bringing about "a wholesale overturning of settled law concerning the religion clauses of our Constitution."[4] They were right. And Congress listened.

WE THE PEOPLE V. WE THE JUDGES

The uproar of negative reaction to Justice Scalia's opinion was deafening. It took three years, but Congress acted decisively to condemn his statist approach through curative legislation. The remedy was brought about in the form of the Religious Freedom Restoration Act (RFRA).

Even though the Supreme Court has the last say as to the meaning of the Constitution, an overwhelming bipartisan congressional majority joined together in enacting RFRA. Passing unanimously in the House of Representatives, and by an almost unanimous vote of 97-3 in the Senate, RFRA sharply criticized the Oregon peyote decision by name and sought to "restore" the strict-scrutiny approach of *Sherbert v. Verner* and *Wisconsin v. Yoder*.

It was an historic first. Religious liberty had never enjoyed such an overwhelming legislative triumph. Never in American history had Congress singled out two constitutional law cases and, in both legal and practical effect, legislatively restored their rulings. It bears emphasis that the cited rulings, Adell Sherbert's and Jonas Yoder's victories, hailed from the 1960s and 1970s and represented (as we saw earlier in the book) full-throated vindications of the free exercise of religion.

Congress had sent Justice Scalia to the legislative doghouse.

In a nippy but sun-dappled Rose Garden ceremony in November 1993, President Bill Clinton signed RFRA into law. It was a cause for thanksgiving, almost on the very day of national celebration.

So, why did Justice Scalia abruptly turn his back on serious claims of free exercise? Wasn't this great justice, so influential during his three decades of rightly-heralded service on the court, a true friend of religious liberty?

The good news is that the answer is not hard to find. And the answer is "yes, he was." With a judicial track record of supporting constitutional values of religious freedom, Justice Scalia had not undergone a sudden change in judicial philosophy.

To the contrary, throughout his distinguished career on the high court, Justice Scalia feared the exercise of judicial power and the resulting displacement of legislative choices. His governing philosophy was simple. Through elected representatives and executive officials, "We the People" govern our own everyday lives. In other words, "We the Judges" should not be making up the rules.

This philosophy, frequently described as one of "judicial restraint," was vividly illustrated in the controversial 2015 case, *Obergefell v. Hodges*, a case mandating same-sex marriage under the Constitution. As Justice Scalia wrote in one of his final opinions, the policy issue itself of whether same-sex marriage should be made legal was not of special concern to him as a citizen.

What was of concern to him? Who is it that gets to decide the issue? Should five lawyers constituting a majority on the Supreme Court strike down what "We the People" had decided acting through legislative representatives (especially in the individual states, since marriage is historically a state and local function)?

In both the Oregon peyote case and in *Obergefell*, Justice Scalia was employing a pro-democracy approach. If the people wanted the law changed, they should go to the state capital and lobby for legislative action. But the people shouldn't expect federal judges to do that legislative job via judicial creativity.

As much as he sympathized with faith communities and their desires to live out and practice their own faiths free from government interference, Justice Scalia had to draw a line somewhere. He drew it at creating judicially-required exemptions from generally applicable criminal laws, laws that applied to everyone without regard to religion. Go to the state capital or to Congress; don't come to the courthouse.

THE RFRA EFFECT—HOW FAR IS TOO FAR

With RFRA on the books, it quickly became evident that Congress had gone too far in determining the legislation's broad applicability. The measure purported to restrain all governments, not just the federal government, and to subject all levels of American government to the exacting constitutional standard of "strict scrutiny."

The law, in a word, applied "universally" to all levels of American government.

But as we saw in the opening pages of this book, Congress can indeed go beyond its constitutional powers, just as the president can. As we described in an earlier hypothetical example, the Legislative Branch cannot simply take over the public-education system of each and every state because, for all its powers, the federal government is limited by our federal structure (as embodied in the Tenth Amendment reserving all non-delegated powers to the states and to the American people) and by the Constitution's specific enumeration of specific (even though broad) powers in Article I.

Congress, therefore, cannot intrude too deeply into the general laws of individual states. As we discussed earlier, Congress cannot, say, govern education or family law or license providers of professional services. It cannot take over state divorce courts or nationalize the driver's license process. The president is likewise constrained, even in wartime or in the midst of the COVID-19 crisis of 2020.

But how to draw the line? What constitutes "intruding too deeply" or "going too far?"

As so frequently happens in our constitutional republic, a local controversy eventually spawned a major constitutional decision that answered these questions. In a case arising in Boerne, TX, a suburb of my beloved hometown of San Antonio, St. Peter's Church, a thriving, rapidly growing Catholic parish, wanted to expand.[5] It sought a building permit from local authorities, but the church was turned down.

The reason, happily, was not secularist hostility or anti-Catholic sentiment. Rather, as a venerable Catholic parish, the St. Peter's Church building had historic significance. It was a local landmark. Local preservation laws led city authorities to reject the Bishop's application which would have altered the physical appearance of the church's historically-significant façade.

Invoking RFRA, Archbishop Flores and St. Peter's argued that the city's rejection of its application failed to pass the highly demanding "strict scrutiny" standard. As important as historic preservation might be, St. Peter's argued, it didn't rise to the level of a compelling governmental purpose. Important, yes, but not "compelling." So, Archbishop Flores argued, the government could not intrude in issues of the church.

RFRA provided Archbishop Flores with a strong argument, but the Boerne city authorities had a better one. To the extent RFRA regulated state and local activity, and therefore prevented the city of Boerne from enforcing its own laws, Congress had violated fundamental precepts of federalism. Specifically, it interfered with the reservation of state power mandated by the Tenth Amendment.

In particular, the city argued, there was no factual basis for Congress to conclude that anti-religious discrimination, in contrast, say, to racial or national-origin discrimination, was a significant issue warranting national intrusion into state authority. Additionally, the federal government had no other justification for RFRA's intruding into the province of the states.

The reform statute was not a regulation of "commerce," a powerful constitutional basis for Congress to act (such as the public accommodations provisions of the landmark Civil Rights Act of 1964). Nor was RFRA an exercise of the federal spending power, the constitutional basis for the Equal Access Act of 1984 (discussed in Chapter 4).

To justify its thoroughgoing invasion into state power, Congress needed to show it was addressing state and local discrimination based on religious belief and practice. If states and localities were engaging in religious discrimination in a systemic way, say in the manner states and localities engaged in racial discrimination, then Congress would have been justified by acting in this federally intrusive fashion.

But under Supreme Court rulings, Congress would have had to build a factual record showing that need in order to justify the intrusion, and that was too tall an order. RFRA was seeking to correct a Supreme Court decision, not to change discriminatory state conduct.

The city carried the day in Archbishop Flores's case. Congress had gone too far. St. Peter's would not be able to expand physically, at least in the way the Archbishop had hoped. Federalism triumphed.

FROM RFRA TO RLUIPA.
IS THIS NARROW ENOUGH?

All was not lost. Congress took the Supreme Court's teaching in *City of Boerne v. Flores* to heart, held hearings in both Houses, and fashioned a more modest but still important law replacing RFRA. The statute has an awkward name and an even odder acronym—RLUIPA; the Religious Land Use and Institutionalized Persons Act of 2000.

Congress obediently heeded the Supreme Court's lesson in *City of Boerne v. Flores*, and substantially drew back the reach of its RFRA-ordained protections. Now, instead of a general law protecting against all actions by states and localities, both legislative and regulatory, Congress took aim at two unrelated but recurring arenas of state regulation: land-use planning (the activity at issue in the St. Peter's case) and individuals institutionalized in a facility that receives federal financial assistance.

In RLUIPA, Congress was careful to ground its legislation firmly in specific, enumerated powers granted by Article I of the Constitution. Both Houses did their homework. Over a three-year period, Congress lavishly documented the grim reality that inmates in state and local prisons faced "frivolous or arbitrary" barriers preventing them from living out their faith traditions.

For example, one state prison in the Midwest refused to provide Muslim inmates with Halal food, while providing Kosher cuisine to observant Jewish prisoners.

In another example, around the country, state correction officials rejected Jewish inmates' requests for sack lunches, which would enable them to break their fasts after nightfall. Unspeakably mean-spirited, numerous prison officials across our country confiscated or damaged inmates' copies of the Bible, the Torah, or the Koran.

Through RLUIPA, Congress meant to put a stop to these abuses.

Why had Congress taken such an interest in the religious practices of inmates? Why had they enacted RLUIPA? In no small part, it was due to the efforts of the late Chuck Colson.

Notoriously greedy for power in his earlier life, super-lawyer Colson served time in prison for his Watergate crimes during the ill-fated Nixon administration. But Colson had a pre-prison "road to Damascus" conversion experience, thanks to the evangelical outreach efforts by a small group of Christian believers in Washington, DC, a group which included a prominent liberal Democrat, Senator Harold Hughes of Iowa.

The progressive Democrat from the Midwest was quite skeptical about the sincerity of the hardened Republican, brass-knuckled brawler's conversion. After all, Colson was a clever, skilled practitioner of electoral dirty tricks.

But Colson's conversion proved to be real, and during his seven-month stint in federal prison, Colson laid the groundwork for what would become Prison Fellowship, a Christian ministry that works to redeem the lives of those behind bars.

As Congress was examining the wreckage of RFRA brought about in the *Boerne* case, Colson (as a Prison Fellowship initiative) weighed in with a controversial idea. Federal religious-freedom protections, he argued, should extend inside prison walls. Congress listened respectfully, then once more acted decisively in favor of religious-liberty values.

With support from the Clinton administration, Congress expanded its post-RFRA focus to include those whom society all-too-often forgets. The House and Senate approved the "restoration" of RFRA. President Clinton, with enthusiasm, signed the measure into law.

Like all good statutes, RLUIPA would be cited, interpreted, and otherwise wrangled with by the Supreme Court in an important case called *Cutter v. Wilkinson*. The court's description should be reassuring to friends of religious freedom: "RLUIPA is the latest of long-running congressional efforts to accord religious exercise heightened protection from government-imposed burdens, consistent with this court's precedents."[6]

Even more noteworthy, this description flowed from the judicial pen of Justice Ruth Bader Ginsburg, a liberal icon who was not widely seen as a friend of religious freedom. That said, careful study of her opinion suggests a much more nuanced (and positive) assessment.

In reviewing Justice Ginsburg's description of RLUIPA, take note again of that final clause which says it is "consistent with this court's precedents." Barring a judicial change of mind (as the court had in *Barnette*) or a constitutional amendment (as with the ten amendments constituting the Bill of Rights themselves), the Supreme Court has the last "say" with respect to the meaning of America's Constitution. Justice Ginsburg was simply recognizing that fact, nothing more, nothing less.

Justice Ginsburg's description is beyond reasonable dispute. Supreme Court supremacy atop Mount Constitution, so to speak, has characterized our system from the outset. It was envisioned by no lesser authority than Alexander Hamilton in "Federalist 78."

During the raging debate over ratification of America's original Constitution, Hamilton expressly envisioned what we call "judicial review." That principle of judicial supremacy—that is, the final say over the meaning of the Constitution—has been enshrined in our law since 1803, first appearing authoritatively in Chief Justice John Marshall's historic and oft-cited opinion in *Marbury v. Madison*. As Supreme Court Justice Jackson would later quip 150 years after *Marbury*, "We are not final because we are infallible, but we are infallible only because we are final."[7]

RLUIPA CHALLENGED

Whenever Congress acts, litigation is sure to follow. And, so it was with RLUIPA. In *Cutter v. Wilkinson*, a diverse group of Ohio inmates, both past and present, filed a lawsuit against the state prison director. They claimed corrections officials in the Buckeye State had engaged in a disheartening variety of anti-religious practices, including denying them access to pastoral care of their respective faiths.

The Ohio prison director responded with the now-familiar defense that RLUIPA may not have exceeded Congress's authority since the state correction system received federal financial assistance, but it was unconstitutional as it violated the establishment clause. After all, could the state be required to provide religious items and meals to inmates?

Although the federal district court in Columbus rejected the state's claim, the court of appeals in Cincinnati reversed it. Why?

The short answer is that the 1971 case of *Lemon v. Kurtzman* struck again (a case we'll examine in Chapter 9), an engine of destruction for claims of religious freedom. Its three-part test: examination of the primary purpose of the statute, its primary effect, and whether it created excessive entanglement between the state and religion, proved fatal in the Potter Stewart Courthouse in downtown Cincinnati.

In the federal appellate court's view, RLUIPA "impermissibly advances religion by giving greater protection to religious rights than to other constitutionally protected rights."[8]

The argument bent logic and common sense. After all, didn't the free-exercise clause by its nature "favor" religious freedom? Of course. That's a fatal flaw in *Lemon v. Kurtzman's* ordained approach.

Recall Chief Justice Burger's opinion in *Wisconsin v. Yoder*, concluding that secularist-based claims for exemptions from mandatory education laws (in contrast to the Old Order Amish's contentions) did not merit stepped-up protection (strict scrutiny) as provided by the free exercise clause. Put simply, the religion clauses of the First Amendment favor religious freedom over secular claims.

As so frequently happens, the lower federal court had arrived at the wrong decision. I say that, humbly, as someone who was privileged and blessed to serve on a federal court of appeals. The truth is, if the final word were left to the regional courts of appeals across the country, or in state supreme courts, religious liberty in America would be significantly diminished, at least on a regional basis.

Thankfully, the Supreme Court once again stepped in and righted the appellate court's wrong. In *Cutter v. Wilkinson*, Justice Ruth Bader Ginsburg, writing for the court, stated, "On its face, RLUIPA qualifies as a permissible legislative accommodation of religion that is not barred by the establishment clause."[9]

Above all, Justice Ginsburg wrote, RLUIPA alleviates government-imposed burdens on private religious exercise. A state prisoner is, by definition, unable to go to church or participate in his local synagogue's worship, but he is still entitled to express his religious beliefs. What's more, RLUIPA did not provide a wink-wink posture of favoritism to one particular faith community over others. To the contrary, the reform measure embodied in RLUIPA simply required government officials to accommodate all religious beliefs and practices, within reason. (We focus more fully on the overarching pro-liberty principle of "accommodation" in Chapter 8.)

The "within reason" caveat is important. The ruling did not require prison officials to stand helpless in the face of unreasonable demands, such as providing Cabernet Sauvignon and steak to adherents of a newly-formed spiritual sect using these elements in their religious memorial feasts.

Also supporting its constitutionality, RLUIPA did not require state or local taxpayers to pick up the tab for prisoners' devotional accessories. That is, corrections authorities may not deny a devout Muslim access to prayer oil, but it could appropriately leave responsibility for purchasing that oil to the prisoner himself. (The ruling in an actual case.) No state subsidies were required.

At day's end, the burden imposed by the pro-liberty federal law was modest and nonintrusive. Justice Ginsburg described the dynamic this way: "RLUIPA [...] protects institutionalized persons who are unable freely to attend to their religious needs and are therefore dependent on the government's permission and accommodation for exercise of their rights."[10]

THE COALITION OF THE WILLING

The Equal Access Act, RFRA, and RLUIPA demonstrate that Congress and the president can be, and frequently have been, friends of religious freedom, even when the courts let us down.

Indeed, the battle for religious liberty can properly be seen as the cobbling together of coalitions of freedom-loving power players and organizations. The opening volley may be fired by one or two leaders in either the House or the Senate, as we saw with the pathbreaking International Religious Freedom Act of 1998, which was pushed by a Republican, Congressman Frank Wolf of Virginia, and a Democrat, Representative Tony Hall of Ohio. The support for that global-reform measure, which created the position of United States Ambassador-at-Large for International Religious Freedom, cascaded through both chambers of Congress and swept westward down Pennsylvania Avenue to the White House.

What was the role of the Ambassador to be? As stated by the Office of International Religious Freedom, the Ambassador was tasked with "promoting religious freedom as a core objective of US foreign policy."[11]

As he had with both the Religious Freedom Restoration Act in 1993 and RLUIPA in 2000, President Bill Clinton signed that congressionally-led, pro-freedom measure into law. To his credit, President Clinton signed the bill with an enthusiastic vote of confidence in its importance for religious freedom around the globe.

The Psalmist famously wrote: "I look to the hills whence cometh my help" (Psalm 121:1). So, too, friends of freedom in our sweet land of liberty can, and should, look both to Congress and to the president for protection of our first freedoms.

In safeguarding America's culture of religious freedom, the Supreme Court does not stand alone. Time after time, all three branches of our federal government do their part to protect religious liberty in the United States and even beyond our shores.

— 7 —

VOUCHERS ON TRIAL

Tommy Thompson, a conservative Republican, was a reform-minded governor of Wisconsin in the 1990s. He believed in traditional Heartland ideals: hard work; individual initiative; and freedom to try. Having served in the Wisconsin state senate, the future presidential candidate and Cabinet officer (under President George W. Bush) knew his home state intimately. At heart, Thompson was an "if it works, let's go for it" kind of leader.

An honest public servant, the governor loved ideas, especially those touching on public policy. He often asked how the government could truly work for the good of the people of the Badger State. As with other great leaders, the governor knew he didn't have all the answers. But he wasn't afraid to explore all options.

Governor Thompson not only wanted smart people of integrity and energy advising him, he was eager to hear policy ideas that promoted human flourishing. He used a single word to encapsulate the idea: "opportunity." Wisconsin should be an "opportunity" state, just as America stood for the vision of an "opportunity society." That, according to the good governor, required freedom. It also required education, which, after all, provided a firm foundation for the exercise of freedom.

Among the enormous obstacles facing the governor was Milwaukee's badly-failing public-school system. Milwaukee's high-school dropout rate was uniquely horrific when compared to the rest of the state. More generally, educational outcomes were abysmal, dropout rates aside. This was the monumental challenge, so what to do?

Embracing the policy research of the Milwaukee-based Bradley Foundation, Tommy Thompson enthusiastically adopted "school choice." Education was, of course, compulsory under state law, but under the school-choice policy, parents were given a say in what school their child attended and students were given the opportunity to attend private schools. Governor Thompson and his supporters reasoned that since public schools enjoyed a government-granted monopoly over education, bringing competition into the system would make all the schools better. He wasn't conjuring this this theory out of thin air. The idea of school choice, as a national education-policy reform, had been pressed by Milton Friedman, a Nobel laureate in economics, in a thought-provoking book, *Free to Choose*, co-authored with his wife, Rose.

But how would parents cope with the enormous financial barriers preventing lower-income students from attending most private schools? The answer, the Governor claimed, was found in a school-voucher system, or in more familiar terms, scholarships. Under the proposal, qualifying families from Milwaukee could secure a voucher, provided at the expense of Wisconsin taxpayers, which could then be used to pay the student's tuition (or at least a significant portion of it) for any accredited school in the city.

Of course, the proposal was met with fierce political opposition from the teachers' union. It warned about the diversion of financial resources from the public educational system. Likewise, the union expressed alarm about the potential "brain drain," with the most academically-promising students exiting the public schools in favor of private (including church-related) institutions.

In a remarkable political achievement, the Governor overcame the union objections and successfully lobbied the state legislature to enact this pioneering voucher program. But the people of Wisconsin would not take the passage of the new law lying down. In fact, they brought a suit that would ultimately bring me into the ornate courtroom of the Wisconsin Supreme Court. The assertion? The pathbreaking school-voucher program violated both the federal and state constitutions.

The theory of the petitioners was straightforward. State taxpayer funds were flowing to private schools, which in Milwaukee (as in most cities) were predominantly religiously affiliated. Specifically, Catholic and Lutheran schools accounted for the lion's share of private elementary and secondary education in Milwaukee. Only a handful of schools were "independent," or free from formal ties to a religious community.

I was deeply honored to be summoned by Governor Thompson to defend the voucher program. So, off I went to Madison, the capital city blessed by numerous lakes and a renowned state university, to meet with the popular Governor.

SCHOOL VOUCHERS. AN EARLY VICTORY

Our initial conversation convinced me that the state's chief executive knew well how to use the levers of power. For starters, the Governor had "fired" Wisconsin's duly-elected Attorney General (and future Governor) Jim Doyle, a Democrat. In Tommy Thompson's view, Doyle could not be counted on to aggressively defend the voucher system in the face of the constitutional challenge filed in Wisconsin state court. So, invoking a seldom-used power, the Governor "replaced" the Attorney General's office for purposes of defending school choice with lawyers from private practice, led by my own Washington, DC-based, law firm, Kirkland & Ellis. Instead of the Attorney General, my partner Jay Lefkowitz and I would serve as the leaders of the Thompson administration's legal team and would defend the constitutional defense in the state's highest court.

As we prepared for the case, our legal team visited "choice" schools. We were deeply impressed. At one elementary school, St. Matthew's, parents spoke in laudatory terms about the school, contrasting it with the nearby public school their children had previously attended. One father said, "at the public school, parents were viewed as outsiders, virtually as intruders. Here at St. Matthews, we are welcome as volunteers. We're able to engage in our kids' education."

The rigor of non-public schools was powerfully illustrated by our visit to Messmer High School, with its charismatic headmaster, Brother

Bob Smith. Kindly and winsome, Brother Bob had built a culture of educational excellence in the context of faithful Catholic teaching. Inner-city schoolchildren were not only graduating at very high rates from Messmer High, they were college-bound.

I sat in on a calculus class and listened as the teacher instructed the students. I quickly realized I was intellectually outmatched, at least as far as numbers were concerned. "I'm glad I majored in political science," I thought. "This is very much over my head." Sure enough, as I spoke with the students, I learned that one of the soon-to-graduate seniors (a school-choice voucher recipient) was headed off to one of the Ivies.

I discovered the students lived in the same neighborhood served by a large public high school. After classes were dismissed for the day, we drove past the high school situated down the street from Messmer High. I'd already reviewed the statistics for that public school. They told a sad tale. The public school's dropout rate was appallingly high, a human tragedy that the governor had taken head on.

The litigation moved quickly, and as it did, Paul Clement, the future US Solicitor General, joined our team. Fresh off a Supreme Court clerkship with Justice Scalia, and new to Kirkland & Ellis, he lent a local touch. By happy coincidence, Paul hailed from Milwaukee, so we were back in his home state. After a full briefing and weeks of prepping for oral argument, I presented our case. By the narrowest of margins, our team prevailed in the Supreme Court of Wisconsin.

Flush with victory, we expected the teachers' union to take the case up to the United States Supreme Court. So it was, but to our surprise, the court exercised its discretion (as granted by Congress back in the 1920s) and "denied cert." In other words, the high court would not overturn the Milwaukee voucher program.[1]

We had prevailed in Wisconsin. The program thus carried on. But, as the policy debate raged around the country about the wisdom and efficacy of school choice, the constitutional issue about using school vouchers to pay for parochial schools festered.

SCHOOL VOUCHERS. SECURING SUPREME COURT AUTHORITY

Out of the blue, I received a call at my law office from the Attorney General of Ohio, Betty Montgomery. With an eye on the Wisconsin experiment, the Ohio General Assembly wrestled with the even more profound failure of the public schools in Cleveland. In contrast to the Wisconsin Supreme Court, lower federal courts in the Buckeye State had struck down Ohio's reform effort on establishment clause grounds. The loss was especially grievous to inner-city parents. One single mom was quoted in Cleveland's *The Plain Dealer*, the city's leading newspaper, as claiming she had graduated from the Cleveland public-school system practically illiterate; she would not silently countenance her own child suffering the same cruel fate.

Like Governor Thompson, Ohio's Attorney General Montgomery, who had formerly been a state prosecutor, was a strongly committed public servant, earnestly seeking to do the right thing for the people of the Buckeye State. She was also firmly committed to her office, which she felt rightly was filled with very able lawyers. In our initial conversation, the Attorney General made two things clear. While my law firm's active involvement in the Cleveland case was warmly welcomed, one of her staff members would argue the case in the US Supreme Court if we succeeded in getting high court review.

That was a strong dose of medicine. Supreme Court advocates, which very much includes those of us who have been privileged to serve as Solicitor General, are eager to face the unparalleled professional challenge and high honor of presenting oral argument in the nation's highest court. Still, I readily accepted the condition. After all, Betty Montgomery was the duly elected Attorney General and her condition was entirely reasonable.

The second condition, which my law firm graciously accepted, was a significant reduction in our ordinary billing rates. Like most states, Ohio was not flush with finances to retain expensive Washington, DC, law firms. In contrast to Governor Thompson in Wisconsin, no

Buckeye counterpart to Milwaukee's Bradley Foundation had stepped up to help defray the expense of an outside law firm.

So, though relegated to a supporting role, our firm rallied to the cause and took an active role in the case titled *Zelman v. Simmons-Harris*. The team, comprising Buckeyes from Columbus and DC lawyers from our Metropolitan Square offices on 15th Street, NW—especially the brainy economist-lawyer Rob Gasaway—worked together smoothly and succeeded in getting a "cert grant." Together, we prepared merits briefs and readied ourselves for the much-anticipated oral argument.

Even with our earlier legal victory in Wisconsin, and favorable if grudging reviews for burgeoning school-choice programs, we knew we faced a formidable challenge. Now, in contrast to the Great Principles of freedom of conscience, noncoercion, free exercise of religion, equality, and non-discrimination, we stared into a virtual constitutional abyss. The arena of public taxpayer support of religious institutions had, over the years, led to a welter of baffling and at times conflicting Supreme Court precedents. We'll enter this thicket more in the following chapter (Chapter 8), but to foreshadow that more-detailed discussion please know this: whether public taxes could go to religious institutions was an area of high court struggle and doctrinal disagreement. We were in a gunfight in a Wild West battleground.

The oral argument proved to be chaotic, but Attorney General Montgomery's designated champion, Judith French (now a state supreme court justice) was nothing short of brilliant. In fact, former Clinton administration official Walter Dellinger, who had served as Acting Solicitor General (and one of my law school professors), described Assistant Attorney General French's argument, especially her rebuttal, as one of the very finest he had ever witnessed.

As the oral argument unfolded, the court's deep ideological divisions quickly became evident. The substantial unity achieved in other vitally important arenas of religious liberty was clearly broken. In particular, Justice Stephen Breyer (appointed by President Clinton) showed his characteristically pragmatic streak. He fretted about a hypothetical international visitor coming to our shores and finding large amounts of tax dollars flowing to parochial schools through vouchers. Wouldn't that hypothetical visitor believe, the justice inquired, that the government had taken the side of religion, by channeling enormous sums into supporting faith-based education?

In addition, Justice David Souter (appointed by President George H.W. Bush) aggressively questioned the Cleveland program's defenders, including our ally (and a good friend), Solicitor General Ted Olson. The reclusive but charming justice from New Hampshire left no doubt that he was adamantly determined to strike down Ohio's effort to save Cleveland's public schoolchildren from a profoundly broken system.

The argument concluded and we gathered back at Kirkland's law offices. Despite the harsh line of questioning, we were brimming with optimism. As our debriefing unfolded, we recalled Justice William Brennan's famous dictum about constitutional law. "What is the most important rule of constitutional law?" the justice would inquire of incoming law clerks. "The First Amendment?" "The Fourth Amendment's protections against unreasonable searches and seizures?" "The Fourteenth Amendment's protections against actions of the States and localities?" "No, no, and no," Justice Brennan would say. The most important rule in constitutional law was the "Rule of Five." "With five votes, you can do anything," he declared.

Five votes. That's all we needed to assure Ohio and the forces of religious liberty a resounding victory. Months later, five votes were exactly what we got.

Signaling the vital importance of school choice, and of the jurisprudence emerging from the establishment clause challenge to Ohio's program, Chief Justice Rehnquist wrote the five-member majority opinion himself. Skillfully swerving past the hopelessly confusing body of prior Supreme Court decisions relating to government aid to parochial schools (again, a subject we turn to in the following chapter), the chief justice from Arizona (and before that, from Milwaukee, home of the original school-choice program) cast a wide descriptive net, reviewing an enormous body of Supreme Court precedent. But he found what he needed, namely three earlier high court decisions that had approved different forms of parental choice, (that is, genuine or true choice) which resulted in parochial schools or institutions receiving state funds.

The first, *Mueller v. Allen*, involved a state tax deduction.[2] Minnesota enacted a program authorizing tax deductions for various educational expenses, including private-school tuition costs. By a narrow 5-4 margin, the court upheld the program, even though religiously affiliated schools were beneficiaries. The basis of the decision: the state program was one of "true private choice."

Why does that matter?

Consider this potential situation. A state government worker, who has the blessing of independent means, signs over his paycheck (or otherwise contributes the entirety of his or her post-deduction salary) to the church. Further hypothesize that the government employer knows full well that this devout employee engages in this remarkable course of generous giving. No one would seriously contend that, under these circumstances, the government was violating the establishment clause. Why? Simple. The employee, not the government, was making the contribution. That intermediating decision "broke the circuit" between government and church.

That circuit-breaking concept carried the day several years earlier in a decision that, surprisingly, brought all nine justices together. In *Witters v. Washington Dept. of Services for the Blind*, the court, speaking through Justice Thurgood Marshall, concluded that the establishment clause did not prevent Washington State from providing financial vocational assistance to a blind individual who sought to study at a Christian college to become a pastor.[3] Key to the decision was that the individual had chosen a field of accredited education. This was "true private choice," not governmental steering, much less coercion.

In the final case relied upon by Chief Justice Rehnquist, the court, by a razor-thin 5-4 margin, upheld an Arizona state program that provided an interpreter to a hearing-impaired child at a deeply Catholic secondary school.[4] Once again, the critical element in sustaining the program's constitutionality was that the student, James Zobrest, made the educational choice freely, with no state coercion or influence guiding his decision.

Those three cases, which spanned the course of a decade, pointed the way for Ohio's victory in the school-choice case.

The chief justice's well-reasoned opinion represented an enormous victory for religious liberty. As Justice Thomas captured in his moving concurring opinion (quoting, among other sources, Frederick Douglass), this was a triumph for inner-city parents, not only in Cleveland but around the country where voucher programs were increasingly in vogue and under attack. Justice Thomas (likewise appointed by President George H.W. Bush) wrote this: "Frederick Douglass once said that 'education [...] means emancipation. It means light and liberty.' [...] Today many of our inner-city public schools deny emancipation to urban minority students."[5] The justice from Pin Point, GA, then quoted the Supreme Court's most important decision of the twentieth century, *Brown v. Board of Education*, striking down public-school segregation: "'[I]t is doubtful that any child may reasonably be expected to succeed in life if he is denied the opportunity of an education [...]'"[6] With echoes of that seminal opinion authored by Chief Justice Earl Warren, Justice Thomas closed with this chilling reflection:

> "[U]rban children have been forced into a system that continually fails them."[7]

Did the establishment clause require this opportunity-denying result? Chief Justice Rehnquist, consistent with the Rule of Five, said emphatically not.

Still this issue of tax dollars flowing to parochial schools, even through the choice of individual parents, was unacceptable to four justices. The truth is, it could have easily gone the other way. Why?

Justice Sandra Day O'Connor (appointed by President Reagan in 1981) had joined the Rehnquist decision and in fact cast the deciding vote in favor of school choice. She could have easily gone the other way, though. Over the course of many years, Justice O'Connor, who exuded moderation and common sense, tried to develop a comprehensive, unifying formula to solve establishment clause conundrums. Though she was unable to develop a cogent doctrine to govern establishment clause cases, she wrote a concurring opinion supporting the Rehnquist decision. In her opinion, she wrote: "I don't believe that today's decision [...] marks a dramatic break from the past."[8]

It was not resounding support for the decision. In fact, it sounded somewhat like "damned with faint praise." With that rumination, Justice O'Connor cut against what Chief Justice Rehnquist had set forth in meticulous detail.

Second, pragmatic as she was throughout her distinguished career, Justice O'Connor took a deep dive into the complexities of the Cleveland system's operation, and suggested that numerous nonreligious school choices were, in fact, available to school district parents under the voucher plan. The range of parental choice included "community schools" and "magnet schools." In fact, Justice O'Connor noted that only 16.5 percent of Cleveland's parents opted in favor of placing their children in religiously-affiliated schools.

By any other name, a win is a win and a cause for joyous celebration. We had satisfied Justice Brennan's all-important Rule of Five, but just barely.

THE BOTTOM LINE: ENSURING THE SAFETY OF THE VOUCHER SYSTEM

In the days that followed, we mused on what might have happened had the Supreme Court actually granted review in the earlier Milwaukee school-choice case. Had that happened, the high court would have confronted a dramatically different set of student demographics. Virtually all Milwaukee voucher students, as the numbers showed, attended parochial schools. Perhaps we would have lost the issue by the tragic 5-4 margin as Justice O'Connor might have become, from our perspective, a casualty of her own doctrine.

Sometimes a loss turns out, in retrospect, to have been a win. As one door closes, so another one opens.

Why? Because in circumstances where tax dollars flowed directly to religious institutions (not through private choice), the law weaved by the Supreme Court year after year (at times with Justice O'Connor's vote proving decisive) was excruciatingly complex, the recipient (rightly) of scathing criticism both within and outside the court for its frustrating contradictions.

This body of jurisprudence, as we will see in the following chapter, was not the Supreme Court's finest hour. But in the face of fierce, well-funded secularist forces, school choice in America was now safe, an enormous step forward for religious freedom.

— 8 —

CAN GOVERNMENT PROVIDE FINANCIAL AID TO RELIGIOUS INSTITUTIONS?

"Hi, Ken. This is David." The call was not unexpected. The executive director of the Baptist General Convention and I had been playing telephone tag for two days. He had a quandary, particularly what to do about federal financial aid to religiously affiliated institutions.

The context? The nation was reeling from the deadly effects of the COVID-19 virus. Shelter-in-place orders were becoming routine, and governors and mayors were stepping into leadership roles ordinarily associated with a local or regional natural disaster, such as hurricanes. But COVID-19 had gruesome and explosive nationwide effects, with business closures and layoffs cascading at unprecedented levels. The human and economic wreckage was appalling.

Churches were not shielded from the economic chaos, nor were religiously affiliated institutions such as the Baptist General Convention of Texas (BGCT). Contributions were plummeting, with layoffs of church personnel looming ever larger as church coffers suffered and cash reserves quickly dwindled.

What to do?

The American people looked to Washington, DC.

In response to the economic toll, Congress passed the Coronavirus Aid, Relief, and Economic Security Act (the CARES Act), which President Trump signed into law on March 27, 2020. This unprecedented measure provided a whopping $2.2 trillion of emergency appropriations in response to the profoundly disruptive effects of the deadly global pandemic. What's more, religious institutions could apply.

The BGCT's governing board had already authorized David to apply for relief under the Paycheck Protection Program (PPP), in an effort to protect jobs. Under the PPP, if the employer committed to use at least 75% of the funds to rehire or retain employees, funds would be funneled to qualifying applicants as loans, the majority of which would be forgiven if the employer used the funds correctly. The funds would help, the executive director said, because donations were down and the BGCT served as the functional "headquarters" of thousands of Baptist churches across Texas. But if the application was approved, could he accept the money?

It was an extraordinary question, particularly in light of the religion clauses' value of safeguarding churches' autonomy and protecting religious freedom from governmental controls. As I knew (and you'll see in this chapter), concerns about governmental funding of religious institutions were as old as the republic itself. But now, churches were looking to "Caesar" for financial support. Was this permissible under the Constitution?

My short answer to David was an emphatic "yes." The BGCT could go forward with its application. Why? How could it be permissible as a matter of constitutional law for a church or religiously affiliated entity to seek and receive federal funds, at least under the circumstances created by the COVID-19 pandemic and Congress's response?

In Chapter 1, we discussed the important constitutional principle of church autonomy. Under America's Constitution, government cannot direct church affairs. Officials of the government cannot appoint or regulate the clergy and the like. So why should this "independent" sphere of civil society—churches, synagogues, and other religious institutions—be able to feast at the government trough?

The answer is found in the principle of "equality," which we explored in Chapter 5. Churches are the living manifestation of the free exercise of religion protected by the First Amendment, the sacred result of like-minded individuals coming together voluntarily, without government coercion, whether direct or indirect. The "creation" of a particular church fellowship reflected the confluence of two freedoms, both the free exercise clause and another fundamental liberty in a free society, the "freedom of association."

EQUALITY AND ASSOCIATION

Freedom of association is not expressly identified in the panoply of freedoms protected by the Bill of Rights. Still, the Supreme Court has wisely held, time after time, that the liberty to associate with like-minded individuals is inherent in our constitutional order.

Consider, for instance, civic groups such as the Lions Club or the cheerily named Optimist Club. Consider the Junior League or your local Chamber of Commerce. Don't these groups have the freedom to gather without government interference? Indeed, during his visit to the United States in the 1830s, young French aristocrat Alexis de Tocqueville spotted this associational freedom in American life, and it's still the same today. We congregate together, form religious and civic groups, and carry out shared values and mission statements.

This cultural characteristic, of course, found itself under profound stress during the civil rights era. Some state governments tried to secure membership lists of the NAACP in an effort to persecute its supporters. The Supreme Court took up the issue in *NAACP v. Alabama*, in which the court aligned itself with the forces of freedom and rebuffed these attempted intrusions.[1] The court concluded that the freedom of association entitled an organization to keep its membership lists secret. The underlying rationale? Hostile state governments might well take adverse action against individuals who had joined the NAACP's ranks to fight for the basic civil rights of black Americans.

Think of the combined power of these two rights, the textually enumerated free exercise of religion, and the broad, religiously neutral freedom of association enjoyed by all groups.

Churches are living embodiments of these two freedoms, but from a public-policy perspective they also are employers. Providing jobs that advance these two rights is naturally helpful, indeed necessary, to a flourishing community. Church staff members aren't left to languish on welfare but, to the contrary, they are consumers and taxpayers. (In contrast to churches and other nonprofit organizations that enjoy various tax exemptions, pastors and support staff members pay taxes and otherwise are typically highly engaged contributors to the community.) In order to pay these staff members, though, payrolls must be met. How can that happen if the sources of income, such as tithes and offerings, dry up during a time of national crisis?

From my friend David's perspective, the BGCT was just like any other employer, even though its paid staff supported the mission and programs of Baptist churches around the Lone Star State. He was right, I assured him. It was that shared, religion-neutral dimension of staff payrolls that provided the lawful basis for Congress and the administration to follow the constitutional golden rule of equality. It should treat all payroll-providing organizations, whether for-profit or nonprofit, religious or secular, in the same way. Treating them differently would be a violation of the equality principle, and would discourage freedom of association in the form of choosing employment with a religious institution.

RETURNING TO THE EQUALITY PRINCIPLE

As we saw in Chapter 6, the equality principle, which allowed the students' Bible study club to meet on campus just like secular clubs, meant that the government could have no favorites, nor could it tell law-abiding groups to go away. That meant churches couldn't be favored in terms of payroll protections, but neither could they be treated unfavorably.

The United States Constitution—the oldest in the world—was expressly designed by the founding generation to "secure the blessings of Liberty" to us all.

Leading the nation through the Civil War, Abraham Lincoln became "a theologian of the American idea."

Dr. Martin Luther King, Jr.'s leadership of the civil rights movement was characterized by a strong appeal to Christian values of equality and liberty.

Completed in 1935, the United States Supreme Court building stands as a powerful symbol in favor of "equal justice under law."

The 2012 Supreme Court, pictured here, ruled unanimously in favor of religious liberty in *Hosanna-Tabor v. EEOC*.

During the COVID-19 pandemic, many churches were forced to close, while liquor stores and abortion clinics remained open.

During the pandemic, Victory Church in Tulsa, OK, creatively held a drive-in church service.

The COVID-19 pandemic shut down much of America.

Legislative prayer is a part of America's religious history. Here, Senate Chaplain Barry Black opens President Trump's 2020 impeachment trial with prayer.

Succeeding Earl Warren, Chief Justice Burger (1969–1986) steered the Supreme Court away from a philosophy of strict separationism.

In a significant victory for religious freedom, the Supreme Court upheld, by a 7–2 vote, the right for the Bladensberg Memorial Cross to remain untouched.

With the powerful force of history and tradition supporting their continuation, Ten Commandments monuments withstood a spirited constitutional challenge and still stand today.

The Amish religious community achieved a significant victory for religious freedom, including a form of home schooling.

A series of school-prayer cases caused a national uproar in the 1960s.

New York Times.

NEW YORK, TUESDAY, JUNE 18, 1963.

TEN CENTS

OTE
DAL;
GRIP

HOUSE COMMITTEE VOTES A TAX RISE FOR OIL INDUSTRY

50-Million-a-Year Increase
Backed to Offset Benefit
of Depletion Allowance

By JOHN D. MORRIS
Special to The New York Times

WASHINGTON, June 17 — The House Ways and Means Committee agreed today to raise taxes of oil and gas producers by about $50,000,000 a year.

Reversing an earlier decision, the committee tentatively accepted one of four Administration proposals designed to offset part of the tax benefits available to the oil and gas industry through depletion allowances. It approved a modified version of another.

The actions came as the committee began taking a second look at some of the Administration's tax-reform proposals that it had previously rejected.

Earlier in the day, Secretary of the Treasury Douglas Dillon told the panel, meeting in closed session, that the reforms it had approved so far would net only about $75,000,000 a year in new Federal revenue.

3 Billion Sought

This is only a fraction of the $13,600,000,000 in new revenue sought by President Kennedy as partial compensation for the $1,300,000,000 in revenue losses that would result from approval of his proposals for cuts in individual and corporation income tax rates.

SUPREME COURT, 8 TO 1, PROHIBITS LORD'S PRAYER AND BIBLE READING AS PUBLIC SCHOOL REQUIREMENTS

Saturday Work Ban By a Church Upheld

Special to The New York Times

WASHINGTON, June 17— A state may not deny unemployment benefits to a person whose religious scruples keep him from working on a particular day, the Supreme Court held today.

The 7 to 2 decision was a victory for Mrs. Adell H. Sherbert, a Seventh-Day Adventist in South Carolina. Her church observes Saturday as the Sabbath and enforces the Biblical command to do no work on that day.

Mrs. Sherbert was employed at Spartan Mills in Beaumont, S. C., when the company went on a six-day week in 1959. She was dismissed for having refused to work Saturdays. Other textile plants were on the same work week, and she could not find a job.

South Carolina law denies unemployment benefits to a
Continued on Page 27, Column 7

CITY G.O.P. FACING FIGHT IN PRIMARY

WIDE EFFECT DUE

Decision Will Require Change in Majority of State Systems

By FRED M. HECHINGER

The Supreme Court decision that Bible reading and the recitation of the Lord's Prayer are unconstitutional as part of regular public school devotional exercises will affect 41 per cent of the nation's school districts.

The affected districts are in 37 states and the District of Columbia. Among them are a high proportion of large systems and apparently a majority of schools.

In New York City, the ruling has led to a hurried appeal by Dr. Calvin E. Gross, Superintendent of Schools, to Dr. James E. Allen Jr., State Education Commissioner, for immediate instructions concerning Bible reading.

A conflict between practices in New York State and New York City underscores the general confusion over the controversial issue.

Reading Required Here

Churches Divided, With Most in Favor

By GEORGE DUGAN

Religious reaction to the Supreme Court decision banning formal Bible reading and the recitation of the Lord's Prayer in public schools was mixed but, in balance, on the favorable side.

Representatives of the "main stream" of Protestant thinking, whose views are reflected in the National Council of Churches, hailed the court ruling. Jewish opinion, too, was largely favorable to it.

For the most part Roman Catholics viewed the ruling with alarm, however, and conservative Protestants, members of small fundamentalist bodies or minority groups in the large denominations, deplored it.

There were many persons of all faiths, however, who took a "so what?" attitude.
Continued on Page 29, Column 8

DIRKSEN IMPERILS CIVIL RIGHTS PLAN

2 CASES DECIDED

Government Must Be Neutral in Religion, Majority Asserts

Texts of the Supreme Court opinions, Pages 28 and 29.

By ANTHONY LEWIS
Special to The New York Times

WASHINGTON, June 17 — The Supreme Court decided today that no state or locality may require recitation of the Lord's Prayer or Bible verses in public schools.

An 8-to-1 majority wrote what appeared to be a final legal answer to one of the most divisive issues of church and state. The opinion of the Court was by Justice Tom C. Clark.

Even the sole dissenter, Justice Potter Stewart, said that religious ceremonies in public schools could violate the constitutional rights of dissenters. But he found the record in today's cases inadequate and would have sent them back for further hearings.

The prayer cases were among a dozen decided today

Retaliate
e Retains
port Curbs
ted Press Cablephoto
er Macmillan,
residence. At
mpstead home.

The *New York Times* announces the Warren Court's decision in *Abington School District v. Schempp*, which resulted in fierce public criticism.

Children, including the Barnette sisters, were required to salute the American flag with their arm extended in the 1940s.

Justice Sandra Day O'Connor, the first woman to serve on the Supreme Court, proved difficult to predict in religious-freedom cases.

BOARD OF EDUCATION OF THE WESTSIDE COMMUNITY SCHOOLS (DIST. 66) ET AL. *v.* MERGENS, BY AND THROUGH HER NEXT FRIEND, MERGENS, ET AL.

CERTIORARI TO THE UNITED STATES COURT OF APPEALS FOR THE EIGHTH CIRCUIT

No. 88–1597.   Argued January 9, 1990—Decided June 4, 1990

Westside High School, a public secondary school that receives federal financial assistance, permits its students to join, on a voluntary basis, a number of recognized groups and clubs, all of which meet after school hours on school premises.   Citing the Establishment Clause and a School Board policy requiring clubs to have faculty sponsorship, petitioner school officials denied the request of respondent Mergens for permission to form a Christian club that would have the same privileges and meet on the same terms and conditions as other Westside student groups, except that it would have no faculty sponsor.   After the Board voted to uphold the denial, respondents, current and former Westside students, brought suit seeking declaratory and injunctive relief.   They alleged, *inter alia*, that the refusal to permit the proposed club to meet at Westside violated the Equal Access Act, which prohibits public secondary schools that receive federal assistance and that maintain a "limited open forum" from denying "equal access" to students who wish to meet within the forum on the basis of the "religious, political, philosophical, or other content" of the speech at such meetings.   In reversing the District Court's entry of judgment for petitioners, the Court of Appeals held that the Act applied to forbid discrimination against respondents' proposed club on the basis of its religious content, and that the Act did not violate the Establishment Clause.

Held: The judgment is affirmed.

867 F. 2d 1076, affirmed.

   JUSTICE O'CONNOR delivered the opinion of the Court with respect to Parts I, II–A, II–B, and II–C, concluding that petitioners violated the Equal Access Act by denying official recognition to respondents' proposed club.   Pp. 234–247.

   (a) The Act provides, among other things, that a "limited open forum" exists whenever a covered school "grants an offering to or opportunity for one or more noncurriculum related student groups to meet on school premises."   Its equal access obligation is therefore triggered even if

The Great Principle of equal treatment for religious clubs was firmly established in Bridget Mergens's case.

Bedecked (sans morning coat) in traditional solicitor general garb, the author receives last-minute suggestions from the Justice Department team before arguing in support of Bridget Mergens's effort to launch a Bible study club at her high school.

Congressman Frank Wolf (in office 1981–2015) was a highly effective champion of religious liberty over an entire generation.

Justice Antonin Scalia (1986–2016) was a strong supporter of religious-liberty values, but badly erred in the troubling case of *Employment Division v. Smith*.

The 2020 National Prayer Breakfast, where prayer transcends partisan politics. Senators James Lankford (R-OK) and Chris Coons (D-DE) pray for the president.

Ohio's school-choice program survived a ferocious constitutional attack in the watershed case of *Zelman v. Simmons-Harris.*

Wisconsin Governor Tommy Thompson and Mesmer High School Headmaster Brother Bob Smith celebrate school-choice judicial victories.

The 2020 Coronavirus Aid, Relief, and Economic Security Act (CARES Act), a $2.2 trillion economic stimulus bill, included churches and religious institutions.

The Spirit of Faith Christian Choir sings at the National Day of Prayer.

Recognizing the role of religious faith in American life, Congress appropriates funds to build and support houses of faith, including the United States Air Force Academy's architecturally-renowned Cadet Chapel in Colorado Springs, CO.

The National Christmas Tree symbolically illustrates the inextricable connection of faith and culture.

A faithful Catholic, Sharonell Fulton has served collaboratively with Catholic Social Services of Philadelphia, which the City of Brotherly Love disqualified from providing foster-child placement.

Founder of Mission Waco, along with his wife Janet, Jimmy Dorrell lives out the biblical admonition to care for the poor, exemplifying the myriad good works carried out by people of faith.

Symbolizing the effort to eradicate religious belief and practice from the public square, a high-school football coach was fired for insisting on praying, alone, after each game.

Jack Phillips of Masterpiece Cakeshop in suburban Denver, CO, fought successfully against state authorities who evinced hostility against individuals of faith.

Ridiculed in the media for his political and religious beliefs, high-school student Nick Sandmann fought back successfully in the courts against powerful media companies.

President Trump announces the nomination of Justice Amy Coney Barrett at the White House.

The Little Sisters of the Poor symbolize the twenty-first century clash between the moral claims of faith and the regulatory commands of government.

Friends of Liberty—carrying on the noble battle to protect and promote religious freedom for all.

Justice Ruth Bader Ginsburg (1993–2020) authored a pro-religious liberty opinion in *Cutter v. Wilkinson*, despite her frequently lukewarm attitude toward religious-freedom claims.

Strangely enough, the simplicity of this unifying answer of equality to constitutional questions eluded the Supreme Court for no less than three decades. In no arena of establishment clause litigation did the court struggle more, or over such a long period, than in the arena of financial aid to religious institutions, especially religiously affiliated schools. In fact, the high court's decisions became a complex web that seemed to defy the twin values that are highly prized in law; logical coherence and predictability of result.

Happily, this multi-decade struggle came to an end with the emergence of Justice O'Connor's centrist leadership. The school-choice cases discussed in the prior chapter provided the intellectual springboard for the equality principle's eventual triumph.

The court's journey began with what should have been an easy case, though it was not. It was a case for the books, the pathbreaking decision holding that the establishment clause, which as we've seen had only been addressed to Congress, could also be applied to states and localities, too.

In the case of *Everson v. Board of Education*, which was decided in 1947, the court identified two overarching principles in dealing with establishment clause cases.[2] Unhelpfully, these two principles pointed in exactly opposite directions, and the bipolar principles were the intellectual weapons wielded by the warring camps in 2020 over the reach of the CARES Act.

To set the stage for our discussion, we travel to the Garden State. A New Jersey statute authorized local boards of education to make contracts for the transportation of children to and from schools. A local township called Ewing authorized reimbursement to parents of expenses for providing local bus transportation to all children in the township, including those attending parochial schools. It so happened that in Ewing all the parochial schools were Catholic.

A local taxpayer vehemently objected to the program. In Mr. Everson's view, the local school board had no constitutional right to reimburse parents of parochial school students for transportation costs. If they wanted to send their kids to Catholic schools, they should pick up the entire tab, including the cost of transportation.

Here, at the headwaters of religion clause streams, emerged the constitutional misunderstanding destined to muddy the waters for decades to come. The notion of equality, of treating everyone alike under the Constitution's golden rule, had not yet dawned on these brilliant justices of unquestioned integrity and ability. Call it a blind spot. Call it a lack of innovative thinking. Call it whatever you want, but the truth was, the justices reviewed all establishment clause challenges through the judicial lens of whether the government participated in the forbidden practice of giving "aid to religion."

Justice Hugo Black pressed the court to take literally the language of the First Amendment, "Congress shall make no law respecting an establishment of religion." He wrote in a sweepingly broad way for the court's majority, and if you take his opinion at face value it appeared certain that the parochial school parents would start picking up the tab for their children's bus transportation. But appearances proved deceiving. Justice Black wrote, "The First Amendment has erected a wall between church and state. That wall must be high and impregnable. We could not approve the slightest breach."[3]

The justice from Alabama, a man who'd been affiliated with the Klan in his earlier days, invoked Thomas Jefferson, who had penned the now-popular "wall of separation" metaphor during his presidency in a letter to the Baptists of Danbury, CT. What did that mean to Justice Black? He wrote, "No tax in any amount, large or small, can be levied to support any religious activities or institutions, whatever they may be called, or whatever form they may adopt to teach or practice religion."[4] Strong language. It sounded very much like the "no aid, period," approach. Yet, the narrow 5-4 majority did what the court should never do. It said one thing, "absolute separation," and did another.

So, what happened? The careful reader will find the answer in a single word embedded, almost hidden, in the space of two paragraphs in the majority opinion. The word is "neutrality." It's a close cousin of the golden rule of equality.

Having set forth at length the Jeffersonian philosophy of absolute separation, Justice Black cast the judicial eye on the context, that of elementary and secondary education. This bus-fare reimbursement program was "part of a general program under which [the Township] pays the fares of pupils attending public and other schools."[5] This program feature was obviously helpful to parochial school parents. "There is even a possibility that some of the children might not be sent to the church schools if the parents were compelled to pay their children's bus fares out of their own pockets."[6] Put another way, the township was indisputably facilitating the religious-education choice of local parents.

But what about police protection, the justice mused. "[S]tate-paid policemen, detailed to protect children going to and from church schools from the very real hazards of traffic, would serve much the same purpose and accomplish much the same result."[7] Should police officers be forbidden to assist children in route to and from parochial schools?

Employing the rhetorical device of *reductio ad absurdum*, he wrote, "Similarly, parents might be reluctant to permit their children to attend schools which the state had cut off from such general government services as ordinary police and fire protection, connections for sewage disposal, public highways and sidewalks."[8] Removing all municipal services would make it very hard, Justice Black suggested, for the parochial schools to operate. As a practical matter, of course, it would be unthinkable.

Justice Black then opined: "But such is obviously not the purpose of the First Amendment."[9] Rather, what was required was "neutrality." It bears repeating: Justice Black was edging toward a unifying theory of the establishment clause (the golden rule of equality) that was destined eventually to triumph. But where is neutrality to be found in Justice Black's decision? He wrote, "[The establishment clause] requires the state to be a neutral in its relations with groups of religious believers and nonbelievers; it does not require the state to be their adversary."[10]

Justice Black's opinion was prophetic. This "non-adversary" theme looms large in the court's religion clause labors. It is an admirably powerful warning sign to justices eager to enforce what they deem to be separationist constitutional norms, yet wary of extending the logic of those norms to the point where the charge might be laid that "the Supreme Court is outright hostile to religious faith and expression."

Narrowly averting defeat, Justice Black nodded in the direction of ideological "separationism." No funds should flow directly to religious schools, he demanded, but under certain circumstances, taxpayer funds could flow to the parents, who might then pay those sums over to religious institutions. Though unwittingly, Justice Black and the *Everson* majority had planted a seed that, well over a generation later, would grow into vindicating the then-nascent school-choice movement discussed in the previous chapter.

Justice Brennan's magical Rule of Five carried the day, but the four dissenting justices pressed their "no aid, period," ideology in two separate opinions. Justice Robert Jackson, author of the pathbreaking pro-liberty decision in *West Virginia Board of Education v. Barnette* just three years earlier, candidly stated that he had undergone a change of heart during the course of his consideration of *Everson*. "I find myself, contrary to first impressions, unable to join in this decision."[11] At first blush, he had considered the Catholic parents worthy of empathy and understanding, plus the modest amount of government funds involved certainly did not constitute "a serious burden to taxpayers."[12] He "had assumed [the issue] to be as little serious in principle" as the paltry sums at stake.[13] Still, as justices are called upon to do, Justice Jackson thought about the issue long and hard. Though his initial inclination was that the moderate transportation subsidy was no big deal, he confessed that "[s]tudy of this case convinces me otherwise."[14]

The majority, as Justice Jackson saw it, had "advocat[ed] complete and uncompromising separation of Church and State," but the majority's separationist language, he continued, "seemed utterly discordant with its conclusion yielding support to their commingling in constitutional matters."[15] Quoting Lord Byron, he wrote, "[T]he most fitting precedent is that of Julia who, according to Byron's reports, 'whispering, 'I will ne'er consent,'—consented.'"[16] In Justice Jackson's view, the non-establishment principle must not be "circumvented by a subsidy [...] or reimbursement of expense to individuals for receiving religious instruction."[17]

To Justice Jackson, a large gulf separated the court's Jeffersonian rhetoric and the actual result the majority reached. Justice Black and his colleagues were being untrue to the separationist principle they espoused.

In like manner, "separation of church and state" was the overarching theme of Justice Wiley Rutledge's impassioned dissent. He lavishly quoted James Madison, who had long ago decried the idea of "three pence" (essentially, a mere pittance) of taxpayer money being directed to religious institutions. This kind of separationist absolutism would find its way into the jurisprudence of the court for decades to come.

The result of these warring factions' vigorous debate? Stalemate ensued. At times, the separationists were triumphant. But battle after weary battle inexorably pointed to victory by the justices who over the generations embraced Justice Black's concepts of "neutrality" and, as a result, upheld "general programs" not specifically directed toward aiding religious institutions.

THE DIFFERENCES BETWEEN BUSES AND BOOKS

The foundation for sustaining general programs designed to help all students, public and parochial, was mightily strengthened two decades later in the context of a schoolbook loan program. Now, rather than a quirky local bus fare reimbursement program, the far more important case, *Board of Education v. Allen* (1968), involved a statewide initiative in the Empire State.[18]

At issue was a New York law requiring local public-school authorities in every district to lend textbooks free of charge to all students in junior high and high school, regardless of the public or private nature of the schools. Predictably, the measure was challenged on establishment clause grounds because a portion of those textbooks were lent to parochial-school attendees. Once again, the challengers lost.

The reason? In the intervening two decades, the personnel of the court had entirely changed. Justice Byron White, a former all-American football superstar for the University of Colorado Buffaloes and NFL

Rookie of the Year for the Detroit Lions, wrote the majority opinion dispatching the separationist claims.

Relying heavily on the New Jersey bus transportation case, the President Kennedy appointee emphasized the pro-educational purposes undergirding the statute. As with the *Everson* case, the court pointed to the "general" nature of the program. He wrote, "The law merely makes available to all children the benefits of a general program to lend school books free of charge."[19]

Again, like *Everson*, the court in the textbook-lending case embraced the no-direct-funding approach, writing "no funds […] are furnished to parochial schools, and the financial benefit is to parents and children, not to schools."[20] To be sure, the former gridiron star acknowledged, books were a lot different than buses. "Most bus rides have no inherent religious significance, while religious books are common."[21] But the New York program did not loan religious books. Only secular books were approved under the program.[22]

But the separationist challengers had one remaining argument. It was not without force. Classroom education at parochial schools inevitably intertwined matters of faith with the ostensibly secular subjects at hand. Under this argument, a pedagogical perspective grounded in a religious worldview would inexorably find expression in the course of teaching the "secular" subject at hand, whether history or physics or whatever.

As the justices frequently do, they went to the high court closet and pulled out a handy piece of judicial "clothing." They found an earlier decision that pointed the way to a congenial result in the case at hand. Once again, the role of precedent, or *stare decisis*, proved pivotal.

Justice White wrote: "[T]his court has long recognized that religious schools pursue two goals, religious instruction and secular education."[23] He pointed to the iconic decision from 1925, *Pierce v. Society of Sisters*, invalidating aggressively secular legislation in Oregon that, in practical effect, eliminated parents' choice of parochial school education for their children. "A premise of this holding," he wrote, "was the view that the state's interest in education would be served sufficiently by reliance on the secular teaching that accompanied religious training in the schools maintained by the Society of Sisters."[24]

Demonstrating the astonishing vulnerability of religion clause cases to internal clashes within the high court, Justice Black, who was the author of the majority opinion in the bus-fare-reimbursement case, vigorously dissented. The irony was palpable. The majority opinion relied heavily on Justice Black's approach in *Everson*, but now the author of that opinion vehemently rejected its applicability to the New York law.

The reason was that books were considered different from buses. "[U]pholding a state's power to pay bus or streetcar fares for school children cannot provide support for the validity of a state law using tax-raised funds to buy schoolbooks for a religious school."[25] Justice Black continued: "Books are the most essential tool of education since they contain the resources of knowledge which the educational process is designed to exploit."[26]

He embraced the separate dissent of Justice Douglas, who quoted extensively from "secular" books that clearly set forth a faith-centered world view. One provocative example was a book entitled *Adventures in Science* which contained this discussion of embryology: "[T]he embryo has a human soul infused into the body by God. Human parents are partners with God in creation."[27]

Once again, as with the dissent in *Everson*, Madison's "Memorial and Remonstrance" was summoned as providing decisive authority for invalidating the book-sharing practice. Not even "three pence" of taxpayer funds could be commandeered to support the religious mission of parochial schools. Books would inevitably be turned into instruments of parochial education. Still, the separationists would not prevail. The court upheld the New York law.

THE *COUP DE GRÂCE* FOR SEPARATIONISM

As the court struggled with the constitutionality of state programs, Congress and the president got to work. If the court couldn't sort it out, perhaps the government could make it clear through legislation.

So, in 1965, at the urging of President Lyndon Johnson, Congress passed Title I of the Elementary and Secondary Education Act. The law provided generous amounts of federal funds to flow to local education agencies, in part to assist low-income students at risk of failing to meet governing academic standards. Title I funds had to be provided for educational services to all children, regardless of whether they attended public or private schools. That said, the services provided to private-school students had to be "equitable in comparison to services and other benefits for public-school children."[28] Among the early applicants for federal funds was the New York City Board of Education.

From the get-go, the board struggled with how to get the federally-funded services to private-school students. At first, the city's school board arranged to transport parochial school children to public schools for after-school, federally funded remedial instruction. The effort was a flop. As would be noted by the Supreme Court, "Attendance was poor, teachers and children were tired, and parents were concerned for the safety of their children."[29]

What to do?

The school board moved the after-school instruction onto private-school campuses, which was exactly what Congress had contemplated. That effort likewise fell short. Keeping kids after regular school hours proved to be impracticable. There was only one remaining option. Remedial services would be provided to both groups of students at parochial schoolhouses during regular school hours. But this was too much for the separationist Supreme Court, which by a deeply divided vote declared in the case of *Aguilar v. Felton* that the New York City program violated the establishment clause.[30]

What did the school board do in response? It improvised by reinstituting remedial-school programs on public-school campuses. It also created mobile classrooms (vans modified into makeshift classrooms), which were parked near sectarian private schools. What's more, the board agreed to transport private-school students to those mobile classrooms if necessary.

The result wasn't just impractical. It was an absolute mess.

After ten years of maneuvering to comply with the Supreme Court's mandate (in the *Aguilar* case), New York City went back to the Supreme Court and cried "uncle." It needed help.

The court agreed. Justice O'Connor, stepping into the fray to overrule the justices' earlier, rigidly separationist position, wrote, "These '*Aguilar* costs' [...] reduce the amount of Title I money [...] available for remedial education."[31] This, in turn, led the city's school board to cut back on the number of students who received those remedial services.

Here was the heavy, real-world cost of separationist ideology. The message to parents was that if they sent their kids to parochial school, they would suffer from the lack of federally funded services that would otherwise be available to them in public schools. Put another way, they would not be treated equally simply because they'd chosen to place their children in private schools.

Justice O'Connor pointed the way for a new majority. Though the separationist ideology of the court had taken hold, it was now relegated to the dustbin of Supreme Court history.

Canvassing more recent Supreme Court decisions, in particular the series of cases involving school choice (discussed in the prior chapter), Justice O'Connor embraced a practical, commonsense approach to on-campus services. Speaking for a new majority, she flatly rejected the separationist ideology espoused by Justice David Souter (appointed by President George H.W. Bush) in a dissent that echoed the vehement dissents in *Everson* and *Allen* a half-century earlier. In a vitally important passage for the future of financial aid, the justice from Arizona stated: "[W]e have departed from the rule [...] that all government aid that directly assists the educational function of religious schools is invalid."[32] She was airily dismissive of Justice Souter's concerns. They were neither "sensible" nor "sound."[33] Harsh words.

To Justice O'Connor, the law, and especially the law of school choice, had left Justice Souter and the ideology of separationism far behind. They were still living back in a different age.

After years wandering in the wilderness of confusing and conflicting Supreme Court cases, the court struck a powerful blow for religious liberty and stepped away from the doctrinaire approach embodied in the court's previous buzz-saw methodology. That previous methodology, formulated in *Lemon v. Kurtzman*, essentially provided that a government program could not advance religion, even inadvertently. But with this change in the court's direction, all sorts of religious institutions could receive equal access to government programs, so long as those programs were not designed to directly promote religious activity.

It was a huge win for religious liberty advocates, but to understand just how important it was, we now turn to that relic from yesteryear, *Lemon v. Kurtzman*. It's a relic, which ironically continues to haunt the Supreme Court's jurisprudence. The encouraging news? Increasingly, the rigid separationist test set forth in *Lemon* is honored only in the breach.

— 9 —

LEMON'S BITTER MEDICINE

The COVID-19 pandemic of 2020 raged on, with thousands of deaths and the loss of millions of jobs. America seemed much harder hit than China, where the scourge began. White House daily briefings, featuring "America's Doctor," 79-year-old Dr. Anthony Fauci, became a routine part of life. Science and medicine, along with public-health measures like social distancing, became lively topics of everyday conversation in the era of "sheltering in place."

As if calling for a national "timeout" during the crisis, President Trump issued a proclamation during the week leading up to Mother's Day announcing a National Day of Prayer. "Throughout our history," the President stated, "in times of challenge, our people have always called upon the gift of faith, the blessing of belief, the power of prayer, and the eternal glory of God."[1]

The White House service marking the day was beautifully inspiring. After his opening remarks, President Trump showcased a nurse from Charlotte, NC, Brittany Akinsola, who responded to the dire situation in New York City by volunteering at the Samaritan's Purse field hospital in the Big Apple. According to President Trump, "There, she worked thirteen-hour shifts in the intensive care unit for weeks, praying for each patient while giving them the very best care. As Brittany said, 'We just keep sharing the love of Christ through our gifts of nursing.'"[2] The event concluded with the Spirit of Faith Christian Center Choir singing "God Bless America" and "I Lift my Eyes Up."

Believer and nonbeliever alike would have found inspiration in the movingly multi-faith, inter-denominational service. There was only one problem. Under the Supreme Court's 1971 decision in *Lemon v. Kurtzman*, the entire event was flagrantly unconstitutional.[3]

The long-established tradition of a National Day of Prayer constituted a cold-on-the-docks violation of the establishment clause, at least as interpreted by the Supreme Court over the long, agonizing course of a generation. But other expressions of government endorsed prayer did, too.

What expressions?

Consider the traditional opening of the Supreme Court's own public sessions. "All rise," the audience is commanded. "All persons having business before the Supreme Court are admonished to draw nigh and give attention, for the court is now sitting." It's a little formal, to be sure, with archaic language, but no harm done. But then, like a killer bee, the following invocation-like words are uttered: "God save the United States and this honorable court."

This prayer, or prayer-like utterance, is certainly an invocation of God's blessing. What's more, the supplication is pronounced by a high-ranking government official, the Marshal, who is, of course, on the taxpayer rolls. Like the National Day of Prayer, this ceremonial opening of the court, to the extent it invokes God's blessing on court and country, violates *Lemon v. Kurtzman's* teaching.

Lemon's potential casualty list is depressingly long. We've already seen (in Chapter 1) that the unbroken Congressional tradition of paid chaplaincies and legislative prayer would fall if *Lemon v. Kurtzman's* three-part test were applied. In his dissenting opinion in that case (*Marsh v. Chambers*), Justice Brennan decried the majority's upholding the chaplaincy practice as a clear violation of the court's "settled doctrine." In other words, the Supreme Court's opinions interpreting the establishment clause, with *Lemon v. Kurtzman* designated as the clean-up hitter in the line-up, represented the final word on a practice's constitutionality.

Something must have gone wrong inside the court. How could a practice as harmless as the president declaring a National Day of Prayer, or the marshal of the Supreme Court intoning the words "God save," or Senate Chaplain Barry Black's opening prayers during the impeachment trial of President Trump, or many more practices run afoul of the opening words of the First Amendment?

LEMON V. KURTZMAN. A BRIEF REVIEW.

Here's how *Lemon v. Kurtzman* plays out in application. Non-lawyers, fear not. It's easy.

When a governmental practice comes under establishment clause challenge, such as the Bladensburg Cross or chaplaincy prayers, the *Lemon* test poses three questions. First, what is the primary purpose of the practice? Second, what are its primary effects? Third, and finally, does the practice entangle government with religion?

The first question is a killer. How can a National Day of Prayer be considered anything other than a national invocation of God's blessing and mercy? Ditto for legislative chaplains. Their primary purpose is indisputably religious in nature, to honor God and beseech His blessings on the nation and (with legislative prayer) the country's elected representatives.

How about Congress's amending the Pledge of Allegiance in the 1950s to include the words "under God"? Under *Lemon*, that becomes very suspicious. What, again, was the primary purpose of the additional words if not to honor God?

Lemon v. Kurtzman is a legal wrecking ball, crashing into long-standing practices and leaving destruction and debris in its wake.

This fatal-like quality has not gone unnoticed inside the court itself. At different times, a majority of justices have cried "Enough already!" "Let's be done with this quarrelsome case." At other times, as in the legislative chaplaincy case, *Lemon* has been treated like a jurisprudential unruly child. Just ignore it, and maybe it will go away. Either way, the *Lemon* test has suffered a sort of demise, only to resurface at inopportune times.

How?

A quick reminder to set the stage. In Chapter 6 on the equality principle, we described the effort by an evangelical church, Lamb's Chapel, to display a James Dobson film series on the premises of a public school (as an after-hours community gathering). In unanimously upholding the church's constitutional right to get access to the school, the court applied the *Lemon v. Kurtzman* test and concluded that the practice, all things considered, was not invalidated under *Lemon's* three killer questions.

In his concurring opinion agreeing with the result, Justice Scalia was in high dudgeon about the court's trotting out the severely criticized *Lemon* test, even in the course of upholding the church's right of access to public-school premises. He wrote:

> Like some ghoul in a late-night horror movie that repeatedly sits up in its grave and shuffles abroad, after being repeatedly killed and buried, *Lemon* stalks our establishment clause jurisprudence once again, frightening the little children and school attorneys of [the town]. Its most recent burial, only last Term, was, to be sure, not fully six-feet under. [...] Over the years, [...] no fewer than five of the currently sitting justices have, in their own opinions, personally driven pencils through the creature's heart.[4]

His colorful language was to little avail. *Lemon* continued to pop up in the court's establishment clause opinions.

More recently, in the Bladensburg Cross case, Justice Alito, in his concurring opinion, decried *Lemon* as infected with "shortcomings."[5] He wrote, "as establishment clause cases involving a great array of laws and practices came to the court, it became more and more apparent that the *Lemon* test could not resolve them."[6]

The court's new member, Justice Brett Kavanaugh, contended in his separate concurrence in the memorial cross case that the court "no longer applies the old test articulated in *Lemon v. Kurtzman*" and "the court's decisions over the span of several decades demonstrate that the *Lemon* test is not good law."[7]

In like manner, the court's most senior member, Justice Clarence

Thomas, opined that he "would take the logical next step and over-rule the *Lemon* test in all contexts" inasmuch as "the *Lemon* test is not good law."[8]

More colorfully, Justice Neil Gorsuch, President Trump's first appointee to the high court, described *Lemon* as a "misadventure" and claimed that the decision had now been "shelved" by the court.[9]

Not so fast. Justice Elena Kagan, the former dean of Harvard Law School and solicitor general, put up a lively defense of the embattled decision: "Although I agree that rigid application does not solve every establishment clause problem, I think that test's focus on purpose and effect is crucial in evaluating government action in this sphere."[10]

So, after fifty years, *Lemon v. Kurtzman* remains on the books. Lawyers, judges, and ultimately citizens have to consider it in assessing the lawfulness of a proposed action that might implicate the establishment clause.

So, how did all this confusion begin? And, going forward, how should law-abiding churches, pastors, and religiously affiliated institutions evaluate new laws, regulations, and state actions?

Let's begin at the beginning. We turn the pages of history back to *Lemon v. Kurtzman* itself.

THE CONTEXT OF WANING LAW

The context was a familiar one. Across the country, elementary- and secondary-education systems were struggling both academically, and for private schools (including parochial schools), financially. Two states, Rhode Island and Pennsylvania, had come up with proposed solutions to address this increasingly intractable issue.

Rhode Island's approach was simple. In its Salary Supplement Act, passed by the Ocean State's legislature in 1969, state education officials were authorized to supplement the salaries of secular, not religious, subjects in religiously affiliated elementary schools. Under the law, the state would pay directly to a non-public schoolteacher an amount not to exceed 15 percent of his or her annual salary. To qualify, the recipient was required to teach in a non-public school at which the average per-pupil expenditure on secular education was less than the average in Rhode Island's public schools.

As an extra precaution against establishment clause snafus, a qualifying teacher could teach only those subjects offered in the public-school system and use only classroom materials that were employed in state schools.

As a final element to guard against financing religious education, the teacher had to agree in writing not to teach a course in religion.

Pennsylvania's approach was more complex. The legislature's concern in the Keystone State was a perceived "crisis" in the state's parochial schools due to rapidly rising costs. As with Rhode Island, the state legislature developed a program focused on supporting the secular dimension of religiously affiliated schools' educational efforts. Indeed, the statutory language made it clear that the measures were providing support only of "purely secular educational objectives."[11]

How? The state authorities would enter into contracts with parochial schools, under which Pennsylvania directly reimbursed the private schools for their expenditures for teachers' salaries, textbooks, and instructional materials. To forestall misdirected reimbursements, state officials established various accounting procedures to identify the "separate" costs of "secular educational services." The schools' "separate" accounts were subject to state audits.

A lot of money (in relative terms) was involved. About $5 million annually was sent from Harrisburg's state coffers to (primarily) Catholic schools across the Commonwealth. By the time the constitutional challenge reached the Supreme Court, Pennsylvania had contracts with almost 1,200 parochial schools, boasting a total student population of more than 500,000. In fact, "[m]ore than 96 percent of these pupils attend church-related schools, and most of these schools are affiliated with the Roman Catholic Church."[12]

The constitutional challenges to the two states' programs found their way to the Supreme Court and were decided under one case. The result was *Lemon v. Kurtzman*'s three-part test.

Speaking through Chief Justice Burger, the court struck down the programs of both states as being in violation of the establishment clause. But now, instead of repeating sweeping separationist language that characterized the court's earlier cases (as we saw in *Everson* and *Allen*), the court struck a chord of humility. Chief Justice Burger wrote, "Candor compels acknowledgment [...] that we can only dimly perceive the lines of demarcation in this extraordinarily sensitive area of constitutional law."[13] Well said.

The "impregnable" wall of separation, imagined by Mr. Jefferson and highlighted by the *Everson* dissenters, was somewhat Oz-like. It wasn't even a "wall," much less insurmountably "high." To the contrary. "[T]he line of separation, far from being a 'wall,' is a blurred, indistinct, and variable barrier depending on all the circumstances of a particular relationship."[14]

This was humility, plus.

The language of the religion clauses, the court observed, "is at best opaque, particularly when compared with other portions of the Amendment."[15] In particular, the chief justice focused on the pivotal word "respecting" a religious establishment. "A given law might not establish a state religion but nevertheless be one 'respecting' that end in the sense of being a step that could lead to such establishment and hence offend the First Amendment."[16]

The court, in short, had to cut off religion-related legislative measures at the pass, lest they develop over time into a classic "establishment" of religion, just as the United Kingdom continues to "establish" the Church of England. The court, like most horses, was skittish.

In fairness, the chief justice did not simply "make up" the soon-to-be-infamous three-part *Lemon* test. To the contrary. For the first and second parts, that is, the need for the state's primary purpose and primary effects to be secular, the court drew from the *Allen* textbook case three years earlier (in 1968). Nothing was made up from whole cloth. Rather, what occurred in *Lemon v. Kurtzman* was a borrowing and transplanting instead of "creating" a new test.

So, too, the third and final piece of the *Lemon* matrix was not original. It was taken from the court's decision the prior year (1970) in a case of huge practical importance to churches and other nonprofit, religiously affiliated organizations, the tax exemption case of *Walz v.*

Tax Commission.[17] (We will examine *Walz* in the following chapter.) "[F]inally," the chief justice stated, quoting *Walz*, "the statute must not foster 'an excessive governmental entanglement with religion.'"[18] The three-part *Lemon* test was now in place, innocently erected but destined to wreak havoc for two decades.

Both Rhode Island and Pennsylvania's programs passed the first two parts of *Lemon*'s tripartite analysis with flying colors. No one could reasonably doubt that legislators in both states were focused on education for all children, period. Why, then, ignore the plight of parents and students in parochial schools? After all, as the Oregon case from the 1920s made clear, families were exercising their constitutional rights in choosing a religious-school education. Surely, they shouldn't be penalized for making that choice.

But *Lemon v. Kurtzman* demonstrated that the third part of the test—excessive entanglement between church and state—would itself become a stumbling block to claims of religious liberty. As the *Lemon* Court saw it, the directing of funds toward secular subjects required careful accounting procedures, which in turn would be reviewed and audited by the State.

This arrangement was problematic. "The history of government grants of a continuing cash subsidy indicates that such programs have almost always been accompanied by various measures of control and surveillance."[19]

The irony was palpable. In both programs, the states required careful separation of teaching secular subjects from religious topics. "An eligible recipient must teach only those courses that are offered in the public schools and use only those texts and materials that are found in the public schools."[20] But this admirable preventive measure sowed, ironically, the seeds of the programs' constitutionally mandated destruction. "A comprehensive, discriminating, and continuing state surveillance will inevitably be required to ensure that these restrictions are obeyed and the First Amendment otherwise respected."[21]

The court drew a commonsense distinction between the book-loan case (*Allen*) and the programs embraced by Pennsylvania and Rhode Island:

Unlike a book, a teacher cannot be inspected once so as to determine the extent and intent of his or her personal beliefs and subjective acceptance of the limitations imposed by the First Amendment. These prophylactic contacts will involve excessive and enduring entanglement between state and church.[22]

But that was not all. The court went on to warn about a very different kind of entanglement; political divisiveness. In the inevitable political struggle over government funding, especially under an annual and, thus, recurring appropriations process, the citizenry would inevitably divide into warring factions. "The history of many countries attests to the hazards of religion's intruding into the political arena or of political power intruding into the legitimate and free exercise of religious relief."[23]

To avoid this double-barreled concern about entanglement, the programs had to fall.

LEMON. NOTHING NEW UNDER THE SUN

Looking back over this last half century of religion clause wars, it's easy to see how *Lemon v. Kurtzman*'s test came to be. Chief Justice Burger simply repeated the teachings of *Everson* (the bus transportation-reimbursement case) and *Allen* (the book-loan program), then added the newly minted "non-entanglement" element of the church tax exemption case (*Walz*).

Scripture teaches that there's nothing new under the sun. And, so it was here. *Lemon v. Kurtzman* was simply piecing together and restating the law that had already been set down in the pages of *United States Reports*, the official government publication containing a comprehensive collection of Supreme Court opinions. In other words, *Lemon* made nothing up.

The unforeseen problem was that the three-part test would quickly become a one-size-fits-all, almost mechanical approach that the court employed in totally different contexts. That is, *Lemon* was a product of a particular era, when parochial schools seemed to be falling apart, as opposed to the lighthouses of educational opportunity they were destined to become, as we saw in the school choice-voucher program controversy (Chapter 7).

Lemon stunted the creation of various state programs to aid elementary and secondary education. At the same time, in walking away from the ideology of separationism and the Jeffersonian rhetoric of "high and impregnable walls," the court set its own trap. It didn't think the problem through. What might have served as a useful approach toward the sensitive arena of direct financial aid to religiously affiliated schools grew into an oversized, all-encompassing approach. A moment's reflection would have led to the conclusion that, say, a presidential declaration of a day of prayer during some unthinkable future pandemic would flunk the test. It was a jurisprudential suit of clothes that didn't fit for all occasions.

Here's another irony. The court missed a key opportunity to rein in the soon-runaway approach embodied in the *Lemon* test. In particular, the court could have yelled "not so fast" when the *Lemon v. Kurtzman* approach confronted the recurring issue of long-standing, historically justified practices. It had the opportunity to limit *Lemon*'s applicability to the context of school cases when it considered the legislative prayer case discussed in Chapter 2. But it passed. Justice Brennan, in dissent, decried the majority's vindication of legislative chaplains by saying, in effect: "But wait, this practice of paid chaplains, although dating back to the First Congress and James Madison and all that, nonetheless violates *Lemon v. Kurtzman!*"

Poppycock. History and tradition, especially the country's unbroken practices over our centuries as a constitutional republic, should easily triumph over newly minted constitutional doctrine.

This should be a welcome relief to friends of religious freedom. But the irony of the *Lemon v. Kurtzman* continuing threat to religious liberty and practice should not be overlooked. A three-part test designed to address one aspect of the myriad, complicated issues in the multidimensional intersection of government and religious institutions and practice became an engine of potential destruction. Sadly, it still is today.

Time and again, *Lemon v. Kurtzman* is rolled into action by opponents of any manifestations of faith in public and civic life. Usually, the pro-*Lemon* forces lose; but they don't give up. And they never will.

The good news, however, is that the Supreme Court has almost always found a way out of the *Lemon v. Kurtzman* wilderness. We see that pro-liberty phenomenon at work in the important principle of accommodation. Once again, even with the shackles of *Lemon v. Kurtzman* hindering its way, the Supreme Court has stood time and again as a friend of religious freedom. It has allowed, in various ways, governmental accommodation of religious faith and practice.

— 10 —

BEATING SWORDS INTO PLOWSHARES

The Accommodation Principle

T he Cadet Chapel at the United States Air Force Academy in Colorado Springs, CO, is an architectural wonder. Profoundly sacred, yet widely known, the chapel is the most visited manmade structure in the Rocky Mountain State. It stands as a wondrous reminder of the importance of faith to even our most resolute men and women in uniform. But the chapel's very existence begs a serious constitutional question. How can Congress, consistent with the establishment clause, finance the construction and operation of a house of worship? This is far beyond the modest amount paid to, say, congressional chaplains.

The simple answer is found in the rich word "accommodation." When you hear the word, you might tend to think of hotels or Airbnb locations. Or perhaps you imagine the cheerful host at the restaurant which "recommends" reservations, but which allows drop-ins. "I think," the host says optimistically, "we will be able to accommodate you and your party." Welcome words.

To lawyers and judges, in contrast, the word "accommodation" brings to mind the "public accommodations" provisions of the 1964

Civil Rights Act, prohibiting racial and other forms of discrimination on the part of businesses serving the general public. It was the Colorado public accommodations provision that handcuffed Jack Phillips, the baker of Masterpiece Cakeshop fame, who refused to bake a custom cake to celebrate a same-sex couple's wedding. Yet another legal platform is found in the "reasonable accommodation" provisions of the Americans with Disabilities Act. (We will visit that important civil-rights measure in the following chapter). "Accommodation" is a watchword in many legal contexts, including the context of religious freedom.

In religious-liberty circles, the phrase "accommodation" represents another Great Principle actively at work to protect religious freedom in America. It's a concept that friends of liberty do well not only to understand but to invoke loud and clear when threats emerge to religious faith and practice.

But what does it mean? Consider some examples.

Happily, illustrations abound of government accommodation of religious faith and practice. In addition to military chapels and chaplains, consider Christmas. By law, it's a national holiday. Each year in December, the White House showcases the "National Christmas Tree," and sitting presidents ordinarily issue a Christmas-time message. In celebrating this way, the government is "accommodating" the religiously informed practices and culture of the American people.

Consider Thanksgiving Day, which is also a national holiday. Thanksgiving is far more than the celebration of the harvest. It is a day of giving thanks to God for our nation's blessings. Here again, from the time of George Washington to the present, virtually all our nation's chief executives have issued presidential statements invoking God in some form or fashion.

Thanksgiving and Christmas proclamations illustrate well the core principle of "accommodation." It will do no good for the American Humanist Association (or any other such group) to go to court seeking an injunction against such presidential proclamations or national days off. Likewise, no federal lawsuit to defund the chapels at the nation's military academies and military bases will succeed.

Why?

The core idea is expressed in terms of "accommodation." Specifically, the United States government can and should accommodate the religious needs and expressions of the American people. To "accommodate" is not to "establish" within the meaning of the First Amendment.

The constitutional principle of accommodation is not, as the name tends to suggest, some sort of compromise, a treaty of peace between persons of faith and secular humanists. To the contrary, it is a principle embedded in the text of the Constitution itself.

THE CONSTITUTIONAL UNDERPINNINGS OF ACCOMMODATION

Consider this language from Article VI of the United States Constitution: "The Senators and Representatives [...] and the Members of the several State Legislatures, and all executive and judicial Officers, both of the United States and of the several States, shall be bound by Oath or Affirmation, to support this Constitution." Notice the two options. An officer, on entering his or her high office, can choose to support America's Constitution either by "Oath" or "Affirmation." What does this mean?

Recall the Barnette sisters in the West Virginia flag-salute case. As a matter of conscience, they could not participate in the school's flag-salute ceremony. Likewise, at the time of the Constitutional Convention in Philadelphia, Quaker influence was strong. Unlike most religious folk, Quakers could not in good conscience take any oath other than to God. They could "affirm," but not swear, their fidelity to the new Constitution. The text of Article VI expressly accommodates that religiously informed position of conscience.

The same "accommodation" holds true with respect to the president. Article II, section 1, provides, "Before he enters on the Execution of his Office, he shall take the following Oath or Affirmation: "I do solemnly swear (or affirm) that I will faithfully execute the Office of President of the United States, and will to the best of my Ability, preserve, protect and defend the Constitution of the United States.'" Once again, no "oath" is required. A simple affirmation of those majestic words of fidelity suffices for the "affirming" individual to take on the most important governmental responsibility in the country.

By tradition, the president takes the oath (or affirmation) by placing his left hand on the Bible, typically held by a beloved family member, and raises his right hand, repeating the oath of office. That extra-constitutional practice of placing one's left hand on the Bible gives even greater solemnity to the oath-taking ceremony. The practice has been "accommodated" since George Washington's inauguration in New York City in March, 1789.

Yet another pro-accommodation example is found in Article VI, clause 3 of the Constitution. Specifically, no religious test can be required "as a Qualification to any Office or public Trust under the United States." A judge cannot be asked whether he or she believes in God before being sworn in. The question would be deemed entirely out of order. In fact, if the person administering the oath, say, the chief justice, were to pose the question to a judicial candidate, it would constitute a violation of an expressly pro-liberty/pro-freedom-of-conscience provision contained in the Constitution.

As we have seen throughout the book, America's founders cared deeply about religious freedom, including freedom of conscience. They believed in it so much that they baked respect for minority-faith practices and traditions into the constitutional text itself. Over the years, that principle has played out in the Supreme Court's jurisprudence.

ACCOMMODATION AND SCHOOL RELEASE

The "accommodation principle" is vividly illustrated in the Supreme Court's highly important "school release" case, which once again illustrated the gulf between the "separationists" on the court and what we can now dub the "accommodationists." Once again, over vehement dissenting opinions, the "accommodationists" carried the day.

For context, the case, *Zorach v. Clauson*, was sandwiched chronologically between the bus transportation case (*Everson*) and the book-loan case (*Allen*).[1] At issue was whether New York City had violated the establishment clause by providing "time release" for public school-children to accommodate religious training and instruction at nearby churches and synagogues. Under the program, students would be permitted to leave school early and go to churches or other houses of worship for training in their respective faiths. Carefully monitored, the innovative program was entirely nondiscriminatory, open to one and all, and leave was granted only with parental permission.

Speaking through Justice Douglas, an avowed FDR liberal, the court upheld the program by a slender 5-4 vote. To Justice Douglas, allowing students to leave school grounds for purposes of religious training was simply an adjustment of schedules "to accommodate the religious needs of the people."[2] He penned these memorable words that continue to stand as the law of the land: "We are a religious people whose institutions presuppose a Supreme Being."[3]

Separation of church and state was not meant to be an absolute, even to Justice Douglas. Too much of a good thing (i.e., separation) is no longer good (i.e., it can become discriminatory). "Rather, [the First Amendment] studiously defines the manner, the specific ways, in which there shall be no concert or union or dependency one on the other."[4] Specifically, there can be no union of church and state, as in England, nor could there be any dependency of the church on the government for support, such as coercing attendance, giving tithes, etc.

Over vigorous dissents, the five-member majority invoked common sense. A profound practical and cultural need existed to accommodate religious belief and practice, lest "the state and religion [become] aliens to each other—hostile, suspicious, and even unfriendly."[5]

By way of the opinion, the majority was waving a yellow flag of caution in the direction of the separationist dissenters. The majority's overarching concern? The danger of a hostile governmental posture toward religion. "We cannot read into the Bill of Rights such a philosophy."[6]

What does this mean? Recall the Bladensburg Memorial Cross case from Chapter 2. Requiring the cross to be torn down or transformed into an obelisk would reflect governmental animus toward religion. In essence, the government would be signaling, "we're going to tear down religious symbols and monuments, just like Revolutionary France." That was a bridge way too far for the culturally sensitive majority.

So, how did the dissenters respond? Once again, they returned to the philosophy of strict separationism. In the lead dissent, Justice Black (the author of the bus-transportation case five years earlier) now embraced a full-throated separationist approach and applied it energetically. In memorable language, he wrote, "Under our system of religious freedom, people have gone to their religious sanctuaries not because they feared the law, but because they loved their God."[7]

Recalling his formative years in Alabama, Justice Black wrote:

> The choice of all has been as free as the choice of those who answered the call to worship moved only by the music of the old Sunday morning church bells. The spiritual mind of man has thus been free to believe, disbelieve, or doubt, without repression, great or small, by the heavy hand of government.[8]

New York City's school release program, in Justice Black's view, was in effect one of governmental coercion. Some students remained behind to languish in the schoolroom, while participating students exited the schoolhouse and headed to their church or synagogue as part of the school day.

Note the starkly different ways of looking at the case. To Justice Douglas, New York City officials were simply bowing, as a matter of policy and choice, to the felt religious needs of the community. They were "accommodating" sincerely held religious belief.

Justice Black, on the other hand, believed that Gotham's city government was teaming up with faith communities to corral students into religious training. Let them go after school, the dissenters suggested, but don't use the coercive powers of the compulsory education laws to guide the schoolkids into religious training.

Justice Robert Jackson wrote a separate dissent, in which he crafted an eloquent expression of separationism. From a deeply personal perspective, he wrote: "As one whose children, as a matter of free choice, have been sent to privately supported Church schools, I may challenge the Court's suggestion that opposition to this plan can only be anti-religious, atheistic, or agnostic."[9] Justice Jackson deeply resented Justice Douglas's intimations that the time-release opponents were anti-religious scolds. Quite to the contrary. In Justice Jackson's view, "it is possible to hold a faith with enough confidence to believe that what should be rendered to God does not need to be decided and collected by Caesar."[10] A very nice, biblical touch in championing the cause of rigid separationism.

These were powerfully competing views, mired in sharp and irreconcilable conflict. The deep chasm between the two philosophies proved to be unbridgeable. It boiled down to the elemental question on the Supreme Court: who can muster the necessary votes, and thus satisfy the all-powerful Rule of Five?

ACCOMMODATING PACIFISM

Throughout the modern constitutional era, the accommodationists have prevailed time and again, even in the face of sharply worded charges of the majority's betraying the nation's grand tradition of separation of church and state. In fact, humanist skeptics might argue: "Time and again, the majority simply caves in. The five justices (or the Congress and president) cowardly surrender to the mighty force of prevailing religious sentiments, at the expense of keeping church and state appropriately separate."

The battle's sharp edges between accommodation and separation are most visible in the inherently sensitive setting of public schools. We have seen the conflict put in bold relief in the school-prayer cases and the on-campus Bible-study club controversies. On some of these thorny issues, the democratic process can (and has) resolved the issue, as we saw with Congress and the president joining forces to enact the Equal Access Act to permit the Bridget Mergenses of the country to organize and promote their faith-filled organizations. But no such compromise was ever reached with respect to the core issue of school prayer. Everyone just continued, over the decades, to disagree.

Instead, in that hypersensitive context of public schools, the warring factions seemed to settle on a sort of compromise. They granted protections for students who simply wanted freedom to organize a faith-focused student organization on an equal footing with secular student groups. Again, there was no bureaucratic favoritism, but no discriminatory exclusions either. Put another way, the court accommodated the students' faith. But what about accommodations of faith outside the schoolhouse? What about accommodations of faith in a wartime setting?

As a foundational matter, let's be clear. When it comes to protecting the nation during a time of war, the country's needs are paramount. National protection is so important, in fact, that some governments require every citizen to serve in some way, no exceptions. Happily, in a country of religious accommodation, our elected representatives have never seriously considered going so far in the government's demand for service.

A quick march down Memory Lane is in order. The Civil War ushered in the first national conscription act, with Congress taking over the states' historic role (going back to the American Revolution) in organizing the militia. Famously, the inaugural legislative measure provided an exemption for anyone who could find a substitute or, alternatively, who could pay a $300 fee.

Originally passed in 1863, the conscription statute was soon amended to recognize conscientious objectors to armed conflict. Still, there was a huge limitation to the exception. In order to claim conscientious-objector status, you had to maintain active membership in a religious denomination whose rules and articles of faith prohibited armed service. Moral scruples, without more, would not do.

This exception to conscription represents a classic expression of the core principle of accommodation of religious perspectives. Recall the old wartime posters, with a determined-looking Uncle Sam pointing a finger right at you: "Uncle Sam wants you." Well, if you could prove you were a conscientious objector, you were, in essence, invisible to Uncle Sam.

Year after year, Congress, with the full support of the sitting president, the commander in chief of the nation's armed services, enacted measures designed to protect conscience-based objectors. As a result, many objectors served in the medical corps, or other forms of service that did not involve combat. In World War II, some 12,000 men entered a program called the Civilian Public Service (CPS), which was charged with performing "work of national importance." CPS corps members worked on a variety of projects, such as agricultural, forestry, and conservation efforts, whereas other corps enlistees worked with neglected communities and at-risk juveniles. Many members volunteered to serve in dangerous occupations, such as firefighting, or in neglected arenas of social service, such as mental hospitals. Not only were the CPS members unpaid, their families and churches contributed millions of dollars for their daily support.

Throughout the twentieth century, Congress tethered conscientious-objector status to religious-based beliefs. The anti-combatant perspective, in Congress's view, had to be grounded in belief in a supreme being, thus excluding agnostic and atheistic objectors. The measure also excluded selective objections to combat, namely those whose objection was based on disapproval of a specific war, rather than a commitment to religious-based pacifism.

Building on Congress's foundation, the Supreme Court, as a matter of interpretation of the First Amendment, embraced the idea of conscientious-objector status based on a set of beliefs that holds a similar position in a person's life as a belief in God. The high court did so by expansively interpreting Congress's religious-based accommodation. In the court's unanimous view, the term "supreme being" was to be interpreted to cover all types of faith, and thereby could successfully withstand constitutional attack as favoring religion over irreligion.[11] The court, in short, interpreted the statutory exemption broadly in order to save it.

During the Vietnam War, the court similarly concluded that a conscientious objector could claim that combat-exempting status even if his conviction stemmed from a personal moral code, rather than "religious" training and belief. But the court drew the line at an individual's objections to particular wars, as opposed to scruples against all wars. The draftee in that case, Guy Gillette, claimed conscientious-objector status based on his opposition specifically to the Vietnam War.[12] That selectivity in attitude wouldn't do. The almost-unanimous court concluded that "Congress intended to exempt persons who oppose participating in all war, 'participation of war in any form,' as opposed to scruples about the morality of a particular conflict."[13]

ACCOMMODATING THE GARDEN CLUB; ACCOMMODATING RELIGIOUS GROUPS

Demonstrating again the case-by-case building of a body of constitutional law, the court in Guy Gillette's case pointed to its decision a year earlier in the all-important tax exemption case, *Walz v. Tax Commission*.[14] There, the court unanimously upheld the long-standing tax exemption for churches in part on accommodation principles.

The challenged New York law was narrowly focused. Like its federal counterpart, it exempted from taxation church-owned property used exclusively for religious purposes. Specifically, church school property could remain safely exempt from federal taxation.

Speaking for the court, Chief Justice Burger sought to capture the essence of the religion clauses' purpose and reach: "'establishment' of a religion-connoted sponsorship, financial support, and active involvement of the sovereign in religious activity."[15] This was not that.

Having been appointed to the high court only two years previously by President Nixon, Chief Justice Burger could look back on the struggles over establishment clause doctrine with an independent, fresh eye. He mused that the court had been beguiled into issuing overbroad statements, resulting in the internal inconsistency decried by various justices ever since *Everson* (the bus-fare reimbursement case) had been handed down almost a quarter-century before. Justice Rutledge, the impassioned lead dissenter in *Everson*, was long gone from the court. So, too, had Justice Jackson, author of the most eloquent dissents from cases sustaining financial aid to schools, whether direct or indirect. (Recall that in in *Everson*, Justice Jackson had pithily observed that separationist doctrine should logically lead to invalidating the New Jersey bus-reimbursement program, and ditto for the New York schoolbook loan program at issue in *Allen*.)

With that background, the nation's new chief justice observed, "The considerable internal inconsistency in the opinions of the Court derives from what, in retrospect, may have been too sweeping utterances on aspects of [the Religion Clauses] that seemed clear in relation to the particular cases but have limited meaning as general principles."[16] Politely stated, but underneath the surface of the restrained rhetoric was Chief Justice Burger's searing critique of what the court had written in case after case since 1947.

The religion clauses were not to be read "rigidly," a recurring theme in religion clause jurisprudence. "[T]here is room for play in the joints productive of a benevolent neutrality which will permit religious exercise to exist without sponsorship and without interference."[17]

The chief then used the key word "accommodation" in a highly creative way. Taken together, the two clauses, establishment and free exercise, created an "accommodation" that "has prevented the kind of involvement that would tip the balance toward government control of churches or governmental restraint on religious practices."[18] He saw the court's labors, metaphorically, as walking a "tightrope." But the court hadn't slipped and taken a nasty fall. To the contrary, "[the Court has] been able to chart a course that has preserved the autonomy and freedom of religious bodies while avoiding any semblance of established religion."[19]

Tax breaks for churches, as the chief justice saw it, didn't "establish" a religion. Such commonplace policies simply treated places of worship the same (recall the "equality principle") as other institutions in civil society. There was no singling out, no favoritism for churches, yet no exclusion of religious institutions, no discrimination. Instead, "[t]he State has an affirmative policy that considers these groups as beneficial and stabilizing influences in community life."[20]

That policy choice was entirely within the state's prerogative. The Garden Club was good for the community; so, too, were the local church and synagogue.

The accommodation principle, supported conceptually by the equality principle, carried the day. In doing so, the "hands-off" policy with respect to property-tax exemptions further protected a core idea of religious freedom, that of the autonomy of religious institutions which is a fundamental value safeguarded by both the establishment and free exercise clauses that were analyzed in the opening chapter.

These two bedrock principles have stood the test of time in the cauldron of vigorous litigation over the court of the last half-century. They have been buttressed by a foundational idea in American law: stay the course.

— II —

DAMN THE TORPEDOES—
FULL STEAM AHEAD

"*Roe v. Wade* should be overruled," I argued, as the nine justices sat up and listened with obvious concern. The stakes were high. I continued in this vein: "*Roe* was wrongly decided twenty years earlier and has been unsparingly criticized over the years for the weakness of its legal reasoning." The case had compromised our federal system, I asserted, unjustifiably intruding into the proper domain of state regulation.

In short, *Roe v. Wade* created a new constitutional right out of whole cloth, namely, the right to abortion. It needed to be overturned and the issue returned to the states.

In contrast to rights expressly identified in the Bill of Rights, such as our first freedom of religious liberty, we allow "We the People" to debate and decide on many of the great moral and policy issues of the age. Our theory of self-governance is simple. When presented with a problem, Americans will study, argue, and then decide, typically in the context of a state legislature or state supreme court. Sometimes, those decisions relate to deeply moral issues.

Physician-assisted suicide provides a dramatic point of comparison. To decide to take one's own life, in consultation with a qualified physician, poses a profound issue of individual autonomy. If a person of sound mind wants to end his life, quietly, peacefully, shouldn't he or she be able to? Isn't this a powerful moral claim?

Yet, in our country, the profoundly sensitive public-policy decision of whether to allow or forbid physician-assisted suicide is one for the voters. In Washington and Oregon, the procedure is allowed. In the vast majority of states, it is not.

Unlike physician-assisted suicide, abortion is not left to the voters. Why a different rule? Why are states allowed freely to regulate (and forbid) the one (physician-assisted suicide) but not the other (elective abortion)? The court simply said so. Abortion, it held, was a fundamental right of individual autonomy. Physician-assisted suicide was not.

That brought me to the oral argument before the venerable United States Supreme Court. To draw from the Battle of Mobile, we were urging the court to "damn the torpedoes—full steam ahead!" *Roe v. Wade* should no longer remain the law of the land, and it was entirely up to the court that had created *Roe* to "steam ahead" and do the right thing.

Our submission was simple. The court should decide it had been wrong. Indeed, badly wrong. Congress couldn't change the law. The president couldn't cure the ill by issuing an executive order. Even the voters ("We the People") were powerless to change *Roe*'s holding. Rather, nine lawyers, appointed for life, had the nation's most vexing moral issue in their hands. But would the justices take the right step, as we saw it, and correct their constitutional mistake from 1973?

As with other sensitive issues, such as capital punishment, whether elective abortion was sound social policy or not was a matter entrusted to the states and ultimately to "We the People." It was emphatically not, as we saw it, a constitutional right preventing states from regulating an elective life-ending procedure.

We thought we were in the right. We believed our argument was persuasive. But once again, as we had in the graduation school-prayer case, those of us serving in the solicitor general's office had miscalculated.

In that showdown case of *Planned Parenthood v. Casey* in 1992, three justices joined forces to form a decisive coalition that, along with three liberal justices, preserved the "core holding" of *Roe* while rejecting its rigid "trimester" approach.[1] That approach was as follows:

during the first trimester, the decision to terminate the pregnancy was solely at the discretion of the woman; after the first trimester, the state could "regulate" the procedure, but could not outlaw abortion during the second trimester; and, during the third trimester, the state could regulate or outlaw abortions except when necessary to preserve the life or health of the mother. The three Justices (O'Connor, Kennedy, and Souter) steered a middle course, allowing somewhat greater state regulation of abortion while blocking its elimination as a constitutionally protected procedure.

Put simply, they were willing to limit the reach of *Roe*, but unwilling to remedy the constitutional hijacking that resulted from that culture-shaping ruling.

Those three justices changed the future of American constitutional law, but not just with respect to abortion. They elevated to iconic status a simple notion in our constitutional order: "Don't change anything. Stay the course."

This approach seemed terribly misguided. If *Roe*'s trimester approach was so wrong as a matter of constitutional law, why save any of it? The troika's response: "*Stare decisis*."

CASEY AND THE MISAPPLICATION OF *STARE DECISIS*

Stare decisis, the familiar Latin phrase (at least to lawyers and judges), means, "It's been decided." Don't revisit and reverse prior court decisions, except for the most compellingly powerful reasons. The torpedoes may be in the water, but it's "full steam ahead."

The Latin is dense, and laypersons might struggle to sort out what the three justices were imparting. Allow me to shed a little additional light.

The plurality of three justices in the *Casey* opinion quoted the great Associate Justice of the Supreme Court, Benjamin Cardozo, from his iconic study of legal reasoning, *The Nature of the Judicial Process*. Precedent was vitally important, wrote the future justice (in what originated as the Holmes Lectures at Harvard). Case was built upon case, decision upon decision, until a large and impressive body of jurisprudence emerged—say the law of contracts or property or torts. This body of jurisprudence informed the legal decisions that came after.

On reflection, the *Casey* plurality chose a curious point for their embarkation. In fact, they went aboard the wrong boat. Why? Because in his lectures, Cardozo was not talking about interpreting the Constitution at all, also known as the power of "judicial review." To the contrary, the learned justice was writing about how the judiciary weaves the tapestry of the common law, using examples drawn from the law of torts (French for "wrongs"). That judge-woven development of the common law, decade after decade, should indeed be logical and incremental, with deep respect for what has gone before. This is the fundamental basis for *stare decisis*.

Interpreting the Constitution, however, is a totally different enterprise. Why? Because just as a statute can be readily overridden by simple legislation passed by a majority vote, so, too, a common law ruling can be set aside, even if it takes a state legislature and the governor working together.

State constitutional amendments are not required to change the law of contracts or torts. To change a constitutional right, on the other hand, requires a constitutional amendment, an ambitious endeavor to say the least. Therefore, if the nation's high court reads a fundamental right into the Constitution where none otherwise exists, and if it is bound by *stare decisis* to uphold that judicially created right, it will be nearly impossible to put the genie back in the lamp.

Simply put, to the extent additional rights are to be included in the Constitution, Congress (and the states) should amend the Constitution by the process set forth in the founding charter itself.

Biting criticisms were leveled at the *Casey* plurality's "stay the course" reasoning. Chief Justice Rehnquist, who had taken the court's center seat in 1986, emphasized that the plurality opinion chipped away at both *Roe*'s methodology and its result (allowing considerably more state-regulatory authority over abortion than *Roe* itself had allowed). "*Roe* continues to exist," the chief justice wrote, "but only in the way a storefront on a western movie set exists; a mere façade to give the illusion of reality."[2]

Additionally: "The sum of the [plurality's] labors in the name of *stare decisis* and 'legitimacy' is this: *Roe v. Wade* stands as a sort of judicial Potemkin Village, which may be pointed out to passersby as a monument to the importance of adhering to precedent. But behind the façade, an entirely new method of analysis, without any roots in constitutional law, is imported to decide the constitutionality of state laws regulating abortion."[3]

In his colorfully quotable critique, Justice Scalia echoed the chief justice's criticism of the plurality's timorous approach: "The Court's reliance upon *stare decisis* can best be described as contrived. [...] I confess never to have heard of this new keep-what-you-want-and-throwaway-the-rest version."[4]

At bottom, the plurality's rein-in-*Roe* approach (but protect a woman's right to abortion) was informed by political and societal considerations. In fact, the plurality was candid in saying so: "An entire generation has come of age free to assume *Roe*'s concept of liberty in defining the capacity of women to act in society, and to make reproductive decisions."[5] In other words, American culture had adjusted to abortion on demand and the court wouldn't turn back the clock.

However, this culture-shaped reasoning overlooked the raging controversy spawned by the court's pathbreaking decision in *Roe v. Wade*, which stood in stark contrast to such iconic opinions as *Marbury v. Madison* (upholding judicial power to strike down Congressional enactments or presidential actions) and *Brown v. Board of Education* (abolishing government-mandated segregated public schools). Whereas *Roe* had declared a constitutional right by fiat, and by the slimmest of majorities, *Marbury* and *Brown* interpreted the Constitution in unanimous fashion.[6]

THE LEGACY OF *CASEY*

Beyond abortion, however, since *Planned Parenthood v. Casey* was decided almost thirty years ago (in 1992), the court has created a complex body of law addressed to this one single issue: when should the justices overrule one of its prior decisions?

For the past thirty years, this entire judicial question of whether to overrule, or not to overrule, has been rather curious. Throughout its storied history, the court had not played its current Hamlet-like role of the anguished decision-maker in the vast arena that is constitutional law.

In fact, before *Casey*, the court operated differently. In interpreting statutes, as we have seen, the court respected prior judicial interpretations. It figured Congress could step in if it disagreed with an interpretation. But as to issues of constitutional interpretation, the court hadn't shown the slightest hesitation to overrule its prior decisions.

Why? It's not only because it requires a constitutional amendment to overturn a constitutional ruling. Rather, it is also because the justices have taken an oath (or affirmation) to uphold the Constitution; each jurist who ascends the bench thus has the solemn duty to interpret the Constitution faithful to his or her own conscience and judgment.

Otherwise, justices who have gone before are, in effect, ruling from the grave. But after *Casey*, America's Constitution had entered a new era. And we're still there.

In the eye of the cultural storm for the past generation, the justices now ask themselves: "Can I vote, in conscience, to overturn a prior decision interpreting the Constitution, even if I think that earlier ruling was wrong?" This newly minted, supine attitude toward its own constitutional precedent embodied a latter-day revolution in the court's thinking.

Let's return to how it was from the formation of the court in 1789 all the way to 1992, just over 200 years later. Think back to our discussion of freedom of conscience. Only three years after handing down its anti-liberty decision in the Pennsylvania flag-salute case (*Minersville v. Gobitis*), a court supermajority rejected *Gobitis*'s reasoning as well as the result of the West Virginia case, *West Virginia Board of Education v. Barnette*. In fact, writing for the court in the latter case, Justice Jackson didn't engage in handwringing or wallow in indecision.

Unlike his timid successors on the high court during the *Casey* era, he fashioned no complex, multi-part test to determine whether the court should reverse its quite recent ruling about the compulsory nature of a flag-salute ceremony. Instead, his opinion was straightforward: *Gobitis* was wrong, period. It therefore should be overruled.

Why?

The justices in *Gobitis* had deferred to state legislatures in a matter of freedom of the mind and justified bringing the coercive powers of government to bear on schoolchildren and their parents with respect to fundamental matters of conscience.

That coercive intrusion into basic liberty was incompatible with America's fundamental values of freedom. As a result, *Gobitis* had to go.

The *Barnette* court's muscular approach to jettisoning bad constitutional law showed no disrespect to the process of judicial decision-making. To the contrary, the court majority in *Barnette* simply did what the Constitution required the justices to do.

In dispatching *Gobitis*, the *Barnette* court was faithfully following the court's then-uninterrupted approach of trying to reach the right constitutional answer, rather than allowing itself to be shackled by the past (no matter how well-intentioned or high-minded the previous ruling might have been).

Lest you think *Gobitis* and *Barnette* are outliers, consider this eye-popping number: Between 1810 and 2019, the Supreme Court overruled more than 200 of its decisions, in whole or in part. Particularly noteworthy, as those numbers show, the court has historically been willing to reassess precedents that limit freedoms vouchsafed by the Constitution.

To reiterate. Laws passed by Congress are different. If the court interprets a federal statute and gets it wrong, Congress can step in and correct what the court has done. Or, Congress can more modestly say, "If that's what we said, that isn't what we should have said. Let's straighten it out." The Article I branch can then pass an amended statute. It bears emphasis that Congress can bring about the desired correction by a simple majority vote in both Houses. With the president's signature affixed, the corrected version of the measure becomes the law of the land.

Interpreting the Constitution is profoundly different. If the court gets it wrong, as it did in *Gobitis*, only the court itself can change things and make it right (absent a very hard-to-achieve constitutional amendment, as I've already noted). Justice Louis Brandeis, appointed long ago by Woodrow Wilson, put the point well in his latter days of service on the high court. He wrote,

> [I]n cases involving the Federal Constitution, where correction through legislative action is practically impossible, this court has often overruled its earlier decisions. The court bows to the lessons of experience and the force of better reasoning, recognizing that the process of trial and error, so fruitful in the physical sciences, is appropriate also to the judicial function.[7]

That's another way of saying: "When we goof, let's admit it and make things right."

Let's call this the "traditional method," namely, the way the court has historically acted. Surprisingly, that straightforward, duty-focused approach is consistently embraced on the current court by only one of its members, Justice Clarence Thomas, joined with increasing frequency by Justice Neil Gorsuch.

Justice Thomas has put it this way: "When faced with a demonstrably erroneous precedent, my role is simple: we should not follow it. This view of *stare decisis* follows directly from the Constitution's supremacy over other sources of law—including our own precedents."[8] But unfortunately for Justice Thomas, *Casey* changed all that, leaving him as the solitary voice for the traditional method. The traditional approach, embraced by generations of justices and now championed by Justice Thomas, is all but dead.

Part of the explanation for this "don't-rock-the-boat" posture lies in the fact that, in contrast to most of our history, the court is now filled, to a person, with career judges. These days, nominees are not chosen from the Senate, as Justice Hugo Black was in 1937. Nor are they chosen from state political office as Chief Justice Earl Warren, former governor of California (and the Republican nominee for vice president in 1948) had been in 1954. The most recent member of the court to have spent any time in the political arena was Justice Sandra Day O'Connor, who served briefly in the state senate in the Grand

Canyon State. But even Justice O'Connor was a career judge, elevated to the Supreme Court from the Arizona Court of Appeals. She replaced Justice Potter Stewart, an Eisenhower appointee who had served on the Cincinnati city council.

The political giants of yesteryear are long since gone from the court. Politicians or other non-judges need not apply. Virtually every sitting member of the court ascended to the high bench from a seat on a federal court of appeals, especially my old court, the DC Circuit, the modern-day "feeder court" for the nation's highest tribunal. This makes for a narrow set of pre-judicial life experiences. Judicial timidity is thus a new phenomenon, born of what Professor Akhil Amar of the Yale Law School aptly calls "the judicialization of the judiciary."[9]

Constitutional interpretation requires far more than superb legal training and skill; it calls for a guiding philosophy of government, and a deep understanding of the nature of our constitutional republic. Sure, it's better to have gone to law school, especially since much of the Supreme Court's work involves the interpretation of statutes and (at times) the weaving of arcane legal doctrine. But a senator, say, or a governor, both of whose offices deal continually with legislation and legal issues more generally, knows the difference between judicially legislating from the bench and allowing the democratic process in a federal republic to work its will.

So, here we are in a highly "judicialized" judiciary, with a reigning philosophy of "full steam ahead." The torpedoes of better reasoning may be in the water, but the invincible SS Supreme Court Majority keeps throttling ahead. This brings to mind the quip from Justice Robert Jackson: "We are not final because we are infallible, but we are infallible only because we are final."[10]

Scary.

ALL THAT SAID . . .

I did not admire the out-sized role *stare decisis* played in the *Casey* opinion. That said, and quite ironically, this stay-the-course approach is actually very good news for friends of religious liberty.

Why? Because of the Great Principles we have been discussing throughout the book.

To draw from the Psalms, those abiding constitutional principles are founded on "higher ground." They have been carefully thought through by the justices over many decades, with decision after constitutional decision reiterating powerful and unifying principles, such as church autonomy, freedom of conscience, accommodation of religious belief and practice, and the primacy of history and tradition triumphing over doctrine.

These Great Principles are firmly rooted in the history and culture of a freedom-loving people. This being the case, *stare decisis* should lock these constitutional principles firmly in place.

In contrast to these Great Principles, judicially created concepts, such as the much-maligned *Lemon* test or Justice O'Connor's "endorsement" theory, eventually fade like biblical grass in the withering heat. "Doctrines" are not what we are calling "Principles" with a capital "P."

Judge-made doctrines come and eventually go, but the Great Principles endure. They are part of our Anglo-American constitutional culture, with roots tracing all the way back to *Magna Carta* eight centuries ago.

That is cause for genuine celebration and thanksgiving. With an added layer of protection found in the stay-the-course approach, the numerous judicial and legislative triumphs of religious liberty gained over the past half-century-plus are securely rooted to stand firm against the gale-force winds of aggressive secularism and anti-faith hostility.

Let there be no doubt. Those secularist forces are ever mustering, preparing for battle after battle. While friends of religious liberty should exercise cautious optimism about the precedential value of previous religious-liberty rulings, one fight that secularists chose to take on may well prove to be a happy exception to the stay-the-course rule. In a Philadelphia foster-care case now pending in the Supreme Court, the secularists' impulse may well result in the overruling, at long last, of the anti-liberty decision in *Employment Division v. Smith* (the Oregon peyote case that we discussed in Chapter 5).[11]

To recap: Congress and the president sought to "overrule" the liberty-denying peyote decision *vis-à-vis* the enactment of the Religious Freedom Restoration Act of 1993. As we discussed, in their zeal to disavow the peyote decision's methodology, the Article I and Article II branches went too far, and the Supreme Court said as much.

But in the case now pending in the court, however, the stay-the-course approach will be put to a strenuous test.

Consider the background of *Fulton v. City of Philadelphia*. Catholic Social Services (CSS), a ministry of the Archdiocese of Philadelphia, has been serving foster children in that historic city for more than a century. CSS became a foster-parent agency in 1917, long before the city first became involved in foster care.

For more than a half century, CSS has routinely enjoyed an annually renewed contract with Philadelphia's city government to care for foster children. Over that long period, CSS has garnered an enviable record of professionalism and compassionate service, service that has been and continues to be much needed. In the City of Brotherly Love, more than 6,000 children are in foster care, and there are more than thirty foster agencies, including CSS, that contract with the city. Still, Philadelphia faces a chronic shortage of foster homes, including homes for 250 children who are placed in institutions because no foster families are available.

Into the drama stepped the local newspaper, *The Philadelphia Inquirer*. With no complaints or allegations pending against CSS, the *Inquirer* published a news article reporting that CSS did not, as a matter of policy and Catholic teaching, place children into foster care outside traditional family structures. How had they received the information? An enterprising reporter simply made a telephone call about placement policy. CSS was honest. Placements would be made only in traditional family units.

The *Inquirer* article ran, prompting a secularist furor. City officials exploded, rising up in righteous indignation and terminating the long-standing arrangement. Odd, because the position of Catholic Social Services was fully known for well over a century. Yet, in the city's suddenly "enlightened" view, it would not do for CSS to follow traditional Catholic teaching and thereby exclude from eligibility otherwise-qualified LGBTQ parents from securing placements.

Philadelphia thus subjected CSS to a general, neutral principle. No discrimination, period, would be tolerated in the rendering of social services under city contract. There was a terrible irony, though. No LGBTQ or unmarried couples had ever even applied to become placement candidates for CSS to consider.

Never mind that the need for these services for Philadelphia's displaced children was profound. No matter that there were already four different agencies that enjoyed the Human Rights Campaign's "Seal of Approval," which recognized those providers' excellence in serving the LGBTQ community. Though there was, in short, no practical need for the city to do what it had done, it did it anyway.

Who suffered as a result? The children.

Catholic Social Services filed suit seeking reinstatement in Philadelphia's program, but ran into the rule arising out of the anti-liberty Oregon peyote case. To pass muster under the free exercise clause, according to *Employment Division v. Smith*, all Philadelphia had to do was have a generally applicable law that was neutral with respect to religion. That minimal requirement was satisfied by the broad "non-discrimination" mandate the City of Brotherly Love imposed. The requirement applied across the board. No exceptions.

As illustrated by the Philadelphia case, thirty years after it issued from the high court, the Oregon peyote case has recently become an engine of secularist destruction of religious values and practices.

The author of *Employment Division v. Smith*, Justice Scalia, a great human being and superb justice, had badly miscalculated. He hadn't seen this coming.

The good news is yet to come, but it's highly likely that the court will (by June 2021) do what it should have done long ago and overrule *Employment Division v. Smith*, just as Congress and the president tried to do in the early 1990s. Why? Because the doctrine in *Employment Division v. Smith* did not embody a Great Principle. It was a creative but misguided exercise in judicial doctrine, which needs to go away.

The rule of *stare decisis* should now bend. It's my hope the court will say forthrightly, "We were wrong. We hereby overrule *Employment Division v. Smith*."

Taking this approach poses no danger to other triumphs in the never-ending battle for religious liberty. Those hard-fought victories were secured through the emerging clarity of enduring principles that undergird our constitutional order. These Great Principles vouchsafe the grace-filled institutions that make life in America much more caring and compassionate than would prevail in a culture dominated by, say, the American Humanist Association or the Freedom from Religion Foundation.

America's churches and para-church organizations will continue to enjoy the protections of the Great Principles, so long as they are vigilant in doing as the Apostle Paul did and making their "appeal to Caesar."

They will need to fight for the right, both in courthouses and legislative chambers across the nation. They will need to understand and proclaim the Great Principles of religious liberty.

If they do, faith communities in America will continue to have a powerful and inspiring story to share.

— 12 —

RECONCILIATION AND REDEMPTION

The Fruits of Religious Liberty

"What lights your bulb, Angela?"

The question posed by part-time law professor, Bob Goff, caught everyone's attention around the lunch table. Individual conversations stopped on a dime. All eyes were focused on the future *New York Times*-bestselling author.

The successful trial lawyer and beloved teacher was in his element. He was inspiring future lawyers gathered around the dean's conference room table at the Pepperdine Law School, situated in the stunningly beautiful Santa Monica Mountains overlooking the Pacific.

Angela was inspiringly aspiring. She had a heart for the poor. Hailing from a middle-class Latino family in Texas, Angela set her sights on attending the Pepperdine Law School (where I was serving as dean) not because of its extraordinary beauty but because of its ethos—to let the light shine, to let justice flow like a mighty stream.

For the same reason, week after week, Bob Goff motored his way northward up traffic-choked Interstate 5 (the Golden State Freeway) from his San Diego law office. As a Christian institution, Pepperdine University, its law school included, embraced the biblical injunction, "Freely ye received, freely give." That admonition posed the simple question: "What can I do to help a hurting world, including those right here around me?"

Bob's chosen cause was global justice. He often asked, "How do we help countries build a system that delivers justice for their people?" He knew the great stories from the twentieth century: Lech Walesa in Poland; Bennie and, later, Corazon Aquino in the Philippines; Kenneth Kaunda in Zambia; and the emergence of democracy from martial law in Taiwan. He understood well that the leaders of pro-democracy movements in country after country were courageous individuals of strong faith. He heard echoes of Nelson Mandela's tribute to the role of faith in strife-torn South Africa. Mandela wrote: "The Church was as concerned with this world as it was the next: I saw that virtually all of the achievements of Africans seemed to have come about through the missionary work of the Church."[1]

But the faith-informed emergence of democracy in country after country had almost been forgotten in the twenty-first century, especially in the wake of 9/11. In light of the worrisome growth of radical Islam, "religion," suddenly carried a lot of baggage for many Americans.

Bob Goff was undeterred. Why not reach out from the comfort and security of America, this "sweet land of liberty," to countries around the globe? Why not encourage scores, eventually hundreds, of American law students to do likewise? Adopt a country, go there, and serve the cause of justice.

Bob would soon become a renowned motivational speaker, helping men and women chase after their dream, whatever it was. *Love Does*, his blockbuster first book, casts a powerful vision of Christian love translated into action, right here at home and around the world. It was that vision inspired then-Pepperdine law professor and now university president, Jim Gash, to venture to east Africa scores of times to help reform Uganda and other nations' criminal justice systems (and penned a wonderful book, *Divine Collision*, chronicling his spiritual journey).

Love Does was, above all, a call to care deeply about people, to go the extra "biblical mile" on behalf of the less fortunate. It was drawn straight out of the Gospels, in particular the Parable of the Good Samaritan, and the letters to the early churches penned by the Apostle

Paul and James, the brother of Jesus. "Faith without works is dead,"[2] wrote the latter, drawing from Jesus's admonition in the Sermon on the Mount to "let your light shine" and his observation, "by their fruits ye shall know them."[3]

Bob Goff no longer focused his "sermon" on the world, though. He increasingly remained close to home, a life coach to "everyman" in the USA, helping each individual to define a highly personal dream. His organizing principle, and the animating principle of *Love Does*, was this: each of us, day in and day out, is to do "good works," the message repeated time and again by the Apostles and carried on through two millennia of church history.

Situated on that beautiful mountaintop overlooking Santa Monica Bay, Angela, as co-founder of Pepperdine's student chapter of a global justice powerhouse, International Justice Mission (IJM), was on fire to reach out around the world for the cause of justice. That was her dream and she told Bob straight. But you have to start somewhere, not everywhere. Bob Goff decided then and there to help Angela achieve her dream.

Out of that lunchtime conversation in the dean's conference room, Angela became a student leader boldly trumpeting a vision of justice for the people of east Africa. Revolution, entirely peaceful in nature, would be followed by reconciliation and redemption, she believed. So, Angela adopted Uganda. War-torn Rwanda soon followed. Through Angela's leadership, literally over half the Pepperdine student body became dues-paying members of the IJM chapter.

Off to east Africa scores of Pepperdine students journeyed to serve the cause of justice. The mission undergirding their pilgrimage was the call from the prophet Micah: "To do justice, love mercy, and walk humbly with your God."[4] Following Angela's lead, they did just that.

Angela is not only a Pepperdine icon. She is a living parable, embodying the faith-filled commitment to serve, to give, to struggle for justice. It was America's culture of freedom that provided fertile soil for individuals of faith, like Angela, to live out lives of caring and compassionate service. It provides the seed corn for what leading sociologists Robert Putnam and David Campbell describe in their magisterial study of religion in the United States, *American Grace*. Faith, translated into good works, makes America a better place.

THE GIFT OF *AMERICAN GRACE*

In his earlier, justly renowned work, *Bowling Alone*, Harvard's Robert Putnam concluded that participation in the nation's voluntary associations was slowly but surely decreasing. People "bowl alone," a powerful metaphor of early twenty-first century societal alienation. Bowling leagues aside, the decline in such organizations' membership signaled a downward trend in social capital, a vital measure of a society's overall health.

This dramatic shift toward isolation represents a sea change in American life and culture. In the 1830s, de Tocqueville famously noted that Americans joined forces together in an almost bewildering array of organizations and institutions, to serve a common cause or mission. The causes varied but shared a unifying feature, namely to make the community (or society, more broadly) a better, more humane, more just place.

In happy contrast to the growing alienation and anomie of modern urban life, Putnam and Campbell concluded in *American Grace* that, unlike their stock depiction in popular culture, religious Americans make better neighbors by almost every index than their secular counterparts. It is in no small measure the religious folks who help keep the myriad civic organizations up and running. According to the Putnam-Campbell findings, religious Americans are more generous with both their time and money, more trusting in nature, more trustworthy and honest, and even measurably happier than their secular neighbors.

Putnam's and Campbell's research was buttressed internationally by an extraordinary peer-reviewed study entitled, "The Missionary Roots of Liberal Democracy." In a massive, multi-country analysis, Professor Robert Woodberry, a senior research professor at Baylor University's Institute for Studies of Religion, concluded that in various countries, Christian missionaries "were a crucial catalyst initiating the development and spread of religious liberty, mass education, [and] mass printing[.]"[5] Missionaries helped spread democracy, and otherwise improved outcomes in the three broad criteria of human flourishing: health, education, and income.

Since you're reading this book, there's a good chance you've experienced this truth. I know I have. Consider this illustration drawn from my own family's experience. My wonderful son-in-law, Cameron Doolittle, a senior director of the Maclellan Foundation in Tennessee, recently penned a book entitled *Joy Giving*. Written from an evangelical Christian perspective, Cameron relates stories from around the world of faith-filled individuals who have joined a bold global initiative, the Generosity Movement. The Generosity Movement's call is simple: to be generous far beyond traditional definitions of philanthropy. It is unabashedly Christian.

One faith-influenced family described by Cameron embraces the "90-10 Rule." Highly successful in their business, the family members give away ninety percent of their income to worthy causes, living on the remaining ten percent. Call it reverse tithing.

This sacrificial other-directedness is found not only in faith-inspired individuals' treatment of finances. Years ago, responding to specific human tragedies that presented themselves to the staff, our local church in Texas, Antioch Community Church, teamed up with local law enforcement to address the scourge of human trafficking. Susan Peters, the church staff member who responded to the felt need spawned by this appalling crisis, created a nonprofit organization, Unbound, which works to redeem and restore lives of young women who have been, in effect, sold into modern-day slavery.

The group's work has been widely praised as embodying best practices, serving as a model for churches and communities around the country. Unbound began as a church ministry, and then spun off as a stand-alone nonprofit. It is also the name of Susan's emotionally moving book about redeemed lives liberated from the sex trade.

Examples of engaged citizenship abound within faith communities. At our former church in Northern Virginia, McLean Bible Church, clergy and lay leaders concluded that both within the congregation and beyond, families with children who had special needs were going almost entirely unaddressed. It was a problem in the church and the community more broadly. One parent put it this way: "Families who have kids with disabilities are often lonely and drained, as I was." The parents and siblings needed a respite, and the child with special needs likewise needed a respite, a safe getaway from everyday life. The result was "Jill's House," an overnight respite center, a temporary home away from home with trained staff and caring volunteers.

A former member of Congress, Steve Bartlett, co-authored the Americans with Disabilities Act. In the 2020 book, *Jill's House: The Gift of Rest*, author Joel Dillon quoted Bartlett, who pointed to Jill's House as a shining example to communities around the country, recognizing that Jill's House filled a need that no one else was serving. Bartlett's observations were buttressed by hard data. According to the National Respite Coalition, across the country there are nearly 17 million unpaid family caregivers taking care of children with special needs.[6] Just like Unbound, Jill's House is now a stand-alone nonprofit organization serving the entire community.

Even more, consider the response by churches and individuals in the aftermath of the brutal killing of George Floyd in Minneapolis in May 2020. Faith-inspired communities rallied around to help bring about reconciliation, healing, and rebuilding. Across the country, volunteers and churches pitched in not only to clean up debris but to help repair small businesses damaged in the senseless violence that attended all too many of the protests. One volunteer from an Atlanta church said this: "We feel like it's our duty as Christ followers to not only stand up for justice but to also stand up for our city." He continued: "One of the ways we get to express that is by helping to clean up and rebuilding."[7]

Buffalo, NY, resident Antonio Gwynn, an 18-year old volunteer in that city's clean-up effort, gave this simple explanation to CNN as to his reason for pitching in: "People needed to get to work."[8] (One viewer was so inspired by Antonio's example that he donated a new car to the aspiring volunteer.) This "let's pitch in and help" attitude flowed naturally from Antonio's active involvement in his local church.

In the city where the nationwide unrest all began, Minneapolis,

MN, churches redoubled their efforts to provide food to those in need, especially targeting neighborhoods that had become "food deserts." Another Twin Cities congregation, Holy Trinity Lutheran, turned its church building into a medic station.

In the midst of the burning and violent confrontation came voices of justice and reconciliation. In our own community of Waco, TX, peaceful demonstrations calling for police reform were prayer-filled in the spirit of Dr. Martin Luther King, Jr., whose name was frequently invoked. No violence, just reconciliation and reform. Dr. King's twentieth-century cries for justice and freedom, through the avenue of non-violent protest, were drawn directly from scripture.

THE PURSUIT OF HAPPINESS: FAITH POURED INTO ACTION

America's founding generation fully understood the generative dimension of America's faith-shaped freedom culture. One of the first legislative acts of the inaugural Congress, sitting in New York in 1789, was to reenact the Northwest Ordinance of 1787, passed by the Continental Congress under the Articles of Confederation. A key provision of that measure stated: "Religion, morality, and knowledge being necessary to good government and the happiness of mankind, schools, and the means of education shall forever be encouraged."

Notice the tie. The very first word in the statutory provision, "religion," was deemed a necessary element to the happiness of mankind. Echoes rang of the words memorably embedded in the opening passage of the Declaration of Independence, "life, liberty and the pursuit of happiness."

Whatever their personal religious views or faith perspectives, the founders of our country perceived religion as an affirmative social good, contributing to human flourishing. As a practical matter, religious faith, they believed, would be translated into action, into countless good deeds throughout the young country, including what was uppermost in the minds of the Northwest Ordinance's architects, the founding of schools and colleges.

Consistent with this cultural foundation of our country, over two centuries later, Putnam and Campbell concluded that religious commitment creates a positive social dynamic, "an inclination toward altruism."[9] And, isn't this true? America's landscape is filled with living symbols of faith poured into action. Hospitals, children's homes, religiously affiliated schools, all these and more are everyday reminders of religious faith and fervor spurring actions and reforms that make life together in community more gracious and peaceful.

In reflecting on *American Grace* and the countless stories of reconciliation and redemption, think back to our discussion of the Lamb's Chapel case. There, the Long Island church pastor was eager to bring the faith-inspired message of family stability to his largely secular community. Divorce was on the rise. The pastor's view was that in his adopted community outside New York City, the integral family was in dire need of strengthening.

Although at first excluded by city officials from using public-school property, the pastor's community-betterment quest was ultimately and unanimously vindicated by the Supreme Court applying one of the Great Principles that protect religious freedom in our country—equality. The principle, which we call the Golden Rule of American constitutional law, is one we can all understand and explain to our neighbors: "Don't single out religious voices for unfavorable treatment at the hands of government." Put another way (in terms a schoolchild might understand), "Do unto religious voices only as you do to secular ones."

With the constitutional baseline of liberty, supported by the Great Principles of religious freedom, Americans are able to launch their own ministries of care and concern, of reconciliation and redemption. They're able to create the very systems and programs contemplated by the Northwest Ordinance of 1787.

MINISTRIES OF CARE, CONCERN, AND SERVICE

Here in Waco, TX, home of Baylor University, which I was privileged to lead for six years, a married couple serve as inspiring role models of living lives of service. Thirty years ago, Jimmy and Janet Dorrell met as Baylor undergraduates, fell in love, married, and ventured off after graduation on a six-month, low-budget, soul-searching adventure to faraway places.

But they weren't simply in search of adventure, although they had plenty of that along the way. Instead, they were searching for their calling in life. Was the mission field beckoning them? And if so, where?

The young couple's travels convinced them that their "mission field" was right back in their adopted city of Waco. And their ministry was to follow the venerable Christian example of caring for the poor. Think of Mother Teresa (or, in the throes of ongoing constitutional litigation here in the United States, the Little Sisters of the Poor).[10]

Out of the Dorrells' global search emerged the concept of "Mission Waco," which is now a model of Christian ministry and outreach to underserved communities. At every turn, Jimmy and Janet would identify a pressing human need. They would then respond in the Bob Goff spirit of "love does."

Take homelessness. "My Brother's Keeper," a Mission Waco initiative, provides not simply shelter and sustenance for homeless men, it provides pastoral and counseling resources to help bring about restored lives. Demonstrating in remarkable fashion the spirit of giving back, the financially-at-risk residents of "My Brother's Keeper" pool their modest resources to provide financial support to several orphan schoolchildren in Haiti.

Or consider food insecurity. Mission Waco established a fresh-food, price-friendly grocery store in the heart of a Waco neighborhood that had featured only convenience stores, with limited and less-than-healthy food selections, offered at premium prices. To provide employment and skill training for special-needs adults, Mission Waco established a now-highly popular restaurant, the World Cup Café, in an at-risk neighborhood.

The list of Mission Waco's "good works" goes on. Its energetic engagement brings to mind the pathbreaking work of Dorothy Day, the journalist-activist who as a convert established the Catholic Worker Movement, whose various communities each founded a hospitality house to provide shelter to those in need.

By legend, St. Francis of Assisi famously instructed Christians to "preach the Gospel, and if necessary, use words." Though there's some question about whether St. Francis ever said these words, Jimmy Dorrell lives his best sermon by laboring tirelessly among the poor. Of course, he is also a preaching minister, with his spoken sermons carried by loudspeaker over the din of fast-moving I-35 traffic at the "Church Under the Bridge". No capital or building campaigns are necessary. The church's popular worship services are attended by rich and poor alike, including travelers wending their way through Waco toward Austin or Dallas. People from all over the country have taken the exit ramp off I-35, enjoyed free on-the-street parking, and have listened to Jimmy's inspiring sermons which embody clarion calls for caring and compassion.

Ceaseless construction on I-35, including the overhead bridge that provides the name for the congregation gathering every Sunday morning, has temporarily displaced the hearty band of worshipers. They currently assemble (consistent with COVID-19 protective measures) on the picnic grounds of the wildly popular Magnolia complex given worldwide fame by Chip and Joanna Gaines, co-stars of the renowned *Fixer Upper* on HGTV. (They now have their own TV network.) That's right. The Gaineses, who have shared their unprecedented success with the Waco community through many good works, magnanimously offered to host Church Under the Bridge during the I-35 construction.

Not far from Church Under the Bridge resides Baylor's Institute for Studies of Religion (ISR). ISR has conducted groundbreaking studies of the role of faith in prisons and jails. American society's oft-forgotten ones are found behind bars where hopelessness and violence, and more recently, COVID-19, all too often hold sway. As demonstrated, however, by Baylor's studies, even the most violent prison culture can be transformed through the grace-filled intervention of faith-guided organizations.

For violence and degradation, no prison in America rivals Louisiana's notorious Angola, the nation's largest maximum-security prison. Controversially, Angola established an inmate-minister program, which deploys trained graduates of the New Orleans Baptist Seminary in bi-vocational pastoral service roles throughout the prison. Inmates lead their own mini-congregations. They serve in lay-ministry capacities in hospice, cell-block visitation, "sidewalk counseling," and delivering "care packages" to indigent prisoners.

David Green, assistant professor of sociology at the City University of New York writes this about ISR's analysis of the Inmate Minister program's results: "[The Angola study] closely examines how and why a morally elevating combination of religious faith and fellowship can foster the motivation and support for inmates to 'make good,' through a process of self-examination and identity transformation."[11]

Jesus's words about visiting those in prison captured the imagination of Chuck Colson, a former top aide to President Nixon who pled guilty to obstruction of justice in the Watergate scandal that felled the nation's 37th president. Emerging from prison with a new mission, Colson founded Prison Fellowship, which quickly became the nation's largest Christian nonprofit serving prisoners, former prisoners, and their families. Not only did Prison Fellowship spawn powerful stories of individual redemption and reconciliation, Colson's organization became a persuasive advocate for criminal justice reform across the country.

From neighborhoods and communities close to home to the entire world, America's culture of religious freedom has paved the way for a flourishing society. It has provided a platform for living lives of generosity and kindness, of creating nonprofits and ministries that promote the betterment of mankind. The founding generation understood this dynamic of human flourishing, and erected a constitutional structure designed to secure "the blessings of liberty to ourselves and our posterity."

That unifying vision of freedom-at-work continues, even in the troubled second decade of the twenty-first century, to "light the bulb" of millions of men and women, old and young. Protecting and defending that culture of freedom, beginning with the first freedoms vouchsafed by the Bill of Rights, is the bracing but inspiring challenge of our time.

— 13 —

THE RISE OF THE CANCEL CULTURE

In recent years, America has undergone a sea change in culture. We see it all around us. Justice William O. Douglas's famous reflection from the Warren Court years, "We are a religious people whose institutions presuppose a Divine being" now seems very long ago and far away.[1] That observation made sense when America watched *I Love Lucy* and *Leave It to Beaver*, or spent Saturday evening watching Lawrence Welk and listening to "champagne music" from the Hollywood Palladium (where I sat for the California bar exam). More relevantly, Billy Graham was making his mark with massive revivals from sea to shining sea. And though America is still blessed with many talented and inspiring pastors who write best-selling books and are followed assiduously on social media, doesn't the spiritual air in America seem to have changed?

America of the Greatest Generation (and of Billy Graham) is no longer, culturally, the America of the twenty-first century's third decade. No one has yet emerged to speak with genuine moral authority to the entire nation. As a society, we're compartmentalized, sliced, and diced. What's more, outright hostility to faith and the denigration of believers' moral and religious beliefs spills out daily. And it's not just in Hollywood as some politicians might lead you to believe. It's happening all around the country. There is Bible and American flag burning in radical Portland, OR. In Denver, the Colorado Civil Rights Commission has excoriated (and litigated) sincere, humble acts of religious conviction by those like Jack Phillips, the Denver baker who refused to bake a custom cake for a same-sex wedding. This is to say nothing of the snide remarks and cynicism suffered by everyday people of all faiths across the country. Hostility to faith has spread across the nation suddenly and dangerously, like a proverbial prairie fire.

Consider what happened to the Church of the Highlands in Birmingham, AL, a super-mega church with over twenty campuses across the state. Some members gather for worship on far-flung public-school campuses, for which the church pays rent. For years, Chris Hodges, the senior pastor, has encouraged his massive flock to serve the poor, engage the sick and elderly, volunteer in schools and, more recently, to step up its community outreach during the COVID-19 pandemic. Winning plaudits all around, for more than a decade the church has operated Christ Health Clinic, which provides free COVID-19 testing in addition to its normal wide array of health-care services.

"By their fruits you shall know them," scripture teaches, and Church of the Highlands has long abounded in good works. Importantly, the church's wide panoply of social services is available not just for church members, but for everyone in the extended community regardless of their faith (or non-faith) journey.

But never mind all that.

Pastor Hodges had the temerity to follow and "like" two social media posts by Charlie Kirk, president of the dynamic nonprofit Turning Point USA. (Full disclosure: I serve on Charlie's advisory board.) The posts had to do with race, particularly in the wake of the horrific death of George Floyd in May 2020. From his own personal page, Hodges simply "liked" Charlie's posts. The beloved, kindly pastor neither shared nor commented on the posts. He simply clicked the "like" button.

This was the unpardonable sin in the age of both "woke" and "cancel" culture. This one act was roundly condemned by the Birmingham Board of Education, which summarily canceled the church's rental arrangements. School premises were immediately closed to the miscreant church. Following the education board's lead, the Housing Authority of Birmingham voted to exclude church volunteers and clinic workers from reaching out to the needy in the city's housing projects. Consistent with its mission, Highlands' members had long provided—without charge, of course—mentoring, health services, and various forms of community support to the city's poor. Solely due to the conservative pastor's expression of his personal opinion, however, the entire church got the official boot from Birmingham.

Even an abject pastoral apology was to no avail in dealing with Birmingham's outraged power elite. Pastor Hodges wrote, "As a pastor and, more importantly, as a follower of Jesus, I work to consider every action carefully, weigh every word, and be respectful of every person and opinion, as Christ taught."[2] His sorrowful *mea culpa* fell on bureaucratic deaf ears.

What's going on?

THE HARM PRINCIPLE

Cultural and political forces are hard at work to attack and destroy practices and norms that have traditionally stood not only unchallenged in this sweet land of liberty but heralded with high praise. It's one thing to tear down monuments of Confederate generals, as military champions of the unspeakable institution of slavery. Whether you like these desecrations or not, that reaction is understandable, albeit lawless. It's quite another thing to decapitate a statue of Christ, which is what happened at the Good Shepherd Catholic Church in Miami, FL. To its credit, the church extended the olive branch of reconciliation, stating "we invite our community to pray for peace." But it was a noble cry for peace when there simply is no peace. American culture is at war, within itself.

The sentiment behind the increasingly venomous attacks on faith is not hard to discern. We can call it the "harm principle." That is, in the views of millions of secularist Americans, religion is now a bad thing. Their reasoning: religious beliefs and practices inflict harm on individuals.

How so?

Faith-inspired people hold to a particular morality and therefore disapprove of acts and relationships that are widely seen in secularist culture as fundamentally important to basic human dignity. If people of faith disapprove of same-sex marriage, for example, secularists believe they are harming individuals of good will, regardless of whether the religious folks unfailingly practice loving kindness toward one and all. A Christian-owned business refusing to provide abortifacients as part of a government-mandated healthcare plan—as Hobby Lobby did—is seen as infringing on women's reproductive rights. To the secularist, the expressions of belief must be rooted out of society's fabric. They must be shouted down.

Let's be clear. In addressing the "harm principle," we're not talking about the horror of sexual abuse by members of the clergy that terribly eroded the moral authority of important institutions and inflicted profound psychological damage on countless victims. Neither are we talking about the numerous acts of hypocrisy and political posturing by those who long espoused religious ideologies. Rather, in this context, we're talking about honest, law-abiding Americans simply practicing their faith and expressing their faith-informed views.

In truth, the true believers in our land of liberty are harming no one. In fact, as we saw in the last chapter, they are helping those around them. Their worldviews are simply offensive to secularists. But although harmless, and indeed, like the Highlands church members, faithfully demonstrating care and compassion, believers are under vigorous assault, simply because they express and act on the tenets of their faith outside home and church, including in their profession.

Let's return to Jack Phillips, the baker who could not in conscience design a cake to celebrate a same-sex wedding. Jack has become a posterchild of the asserted "harm principle." Even though he gladly creates and serves various cake designs for one and all, regardless of sexual orientation, he cannot in good conscience comply with a request to celebrate a same-sex wedding by the creation of a custom cake. He feels this kind of celebration is at odds with his evangelical faith.

In this context, the theory undergirding the "harm principle" is this: by these acts of exclusion, Jack Phillips is inflicting a form of dignitary harm on the lawfully married couple seeking to purchase his specially designed cake. His refusal to create a nuptial celebratory delight becomes, under this view, an intolerable rebuff to basic human dignity.

That's the idea in a nutshell. It boils down, fairly viewed, to hurt feelings. But on reflection, this form of "harm" happens routinely in everyday life.

Consider this verbal assault: "Why are you wearing a MAGA hat? You must be a racist!" Those words are not unknown in the vigorous political battles of our time. Such broadsides cause wounded feelings or worse. Remember Nicholas Sandmann, the Catholic high-school student challenged by a drum-beating Native American activist on the grounds of the Lincoln Memorial? The chanting, in-your-face demonstrator was, it appears, offended by the student's bright red MAGA cap. The media then transformed the confrontation into a national spectacle, condemning in a virtually apoplectic manner the high schooler for his would-be thoughtlessness.

Yet, on reflection, it's obvious that barbs and brickbats are part and parcel of everyday life in democracies where freedom of speech is—or at least historically has been—exalted as a fundamental right.

On careful analysis, the asserted "harm" to individual dignity is by no means the principal "evil" that the secular culture seeks to address and remedy. It's faith, pure and simple, and according to the secularists it must be eliminated from the public square.

Consider the saga of Joe Kennedy, a Marine Corps veteran, who became (as a second career) head coach for the junior varsity football team at Bremerton High School near Seattle. Before he coached his first game, Coach Kennedy made a moral commitment that he would give thanks to God after every game for the opportunity to serve as a football coach, win or lose.

After that first game, Coach Kennedy waited until the players cleared the field, then took a knee and silently thanked God for his players. He continued this quiet, unobtrusive practice for seven years. No players were coerced or pressured into participating in the coach's prayer event. For good measure, it was silent prayer. No one complained. But ironically, a compliment triggered the downhill slide toward the coach's eventual firing.

A school administrator committed the fateful act of expressing gratitude for Coach Kennedy's leadership and the fine example he provided for the team through his post-game prayers. That kudo was too much for school bureaucrats. They fired off what we lawyers call "a demand letter," insisting that the coach cease his prayer practice. This broadside was promptly followed by a zinger missive from the superintendent, instructing Coach Kennedy that he must stop praying after games.

To his credit, Coach Kennedy followed the example of the Apostle Paul as chronicled in the Book of Acts. He litigated.

Reaching out to a leading national religious-freedom defense firm, First Liberty Institute, Coach Kennedy was reassured that he was entirely within his rights as a public employee. He did not have to bow down to Caesar. Seeking middle ground, First Liberty lawyers proposed a compromise. The school district should allow Coach Kennedy to take fifteen seconds after the game and silently thank God for his team, but only when the players were off the field.

The Bremerton school bureaucrats said no. Any violation of the "no prayer" policy "cannot be tolerated," they said. First Liberty appealed to the EEOC to vindicate Coach Kennedy's basic rights; the agency issued the obligatory "right to sue" letter; and the long saga began in the courts. The dreaded Ninth Circuit Court of Appeals, the most hostile federal court to religious belief and expression, ruled in favor of the school district, and, disappointingly, the Supreme Court declined to hear Coach Kennedy's appeal. Instead, they let the anti-liberty ruling stand, without approving of it or otherwise opining on the merits of the case. (In fact, four justices chastised the Ninth Circuit's out-with-religion stance.)[3]

Coach Kennedy's long but continuing march through the federal courts demonstrates two harsh realities. Going far beyond vindicating the "harm principle," the secularist culture will fight to eradicate religious faith and practice from the marketplace. The secularists, in extreme form, will burn Bibles. They will certainly stop prayer, even silent prayer, on bended knee.

Remember the effort we discussed earlier in the book to end legislative prayer. That's just the beginning. Now, recall the challenge to the long-standing memorial cross in Bladensburg, MD. Note that the challenge was mounted by the American Humanist Association, an organization dedicated to purging faith from the public square. These groups are growing in number and in aggressiveness. Though the court rose to the occasion and vindicated our constitutional traditions of protecting religious belief and expression in the *Bladensburg* case, we should not view the judiciary as the biblical "everlasting arms" on which we are to confidently rely. Inevitably, the courts will fail us, as they did in Coach Kennedy's case. Indeed, as the Supreme Court likes to say, we are not a court of "error correction." The nine justices—or any five-member majority of it—cannot fix every problem.

DON'T GIVE UP THE FIGHT

It should go without saying. Friends of liberty must never flag in their zeal to preserve our first freedom. "Cancel culture" is powerful and increasingly relentless. That means, to borrow a phrase, that friends of liberty need to fight back. Or, to borrow from Churchill, we must never give in. All the more so, since enemies of religious freedom are vigorously on the march.

But it is not only religious liberty that's under assault in America. Our entire constitutional order of democratic debate is under challenge.

In a non-faith context, consider the numerous campus incidents in recent years shutting down lectures by "controversial" speakers. Recall the case of Charles Murray, a highly respected scholar at the American Enterprise Institute, invited to speak at Middlebury College in 2017. Refusing to listen to what Murray had to say, hundreds of student protesters (encouraged by some of their professors) disrupted the long-scheduled lecture, turned their backs, and chanted: "Your message is hatred. We cannot tolerate it."

What was Murray's offense? He was thrice "guilty" of unforgivable offenses in modern thinking: "Racist, sexist, anti-gay, Charles Murray, go away." The charges were entirely bogus. The "basis" of this three-count "indictment" was a handful of thought-provoking books, each elaborately documented as befits the work of a leading social scientist and Harvard PhD. His real offense was that he was espousing the "wrong" ideas.

But Murray wasn't just shouted down by the Middlebury mob. He was physically attacked. He later reflected on the incident. "We were confronted by a mob that man-handled us that, had it not been for the security guards, at the very least, I would have been on the ground."[3]

To its credit, Middlebury College took disciplinary action. Sixty-seven students will (presumably) forever have a huge smudge on their records. Instead of confronting speech with speech in a peaceful and respectful manner, these sixty-seven students employed raw power to "cancel" Murray's talk. (Oddly, the local police filed no criminal charges, even though some members of the mob engaged in physical assault.)

Like spring, "cancel culture" arrived early in New England. And its message was clear: "I disagree with what you say, and I'm going to prevent you from saying it."

But it wasn't always this way. This is a new-born, anti-liberty heresy.

Allow me the luxury of marching, briefly, down Memory Lane (one of my favorite streets). During my college years, in the tumultuous Sixties no less, I spent two wonderful summers at the Harvard summer school—my modest version of "a Harvard education." During my first summer, a controversial speaker came to campus. William Styron, a leading novelist of the time, had recently published a blockbuster best-seller, the widely acclaimed *Confessions of Nat Turner*. It was an extraordinary book, a form of historical fiction based on a bloody, pre-Civil War slave revolt in Virginia led by freedom-fighter and slave fugitive, Nat Turner. To a packed audience, Styron spoke at length. Then, the eagerly anticipated Q & A session began. The questions flowing from the audience were bitterly hostile. Particularly forceful in tone, students of color posed question after question to the following effect: "How could you, a white man, have the temerity to write as if you were black, and a fugitive slave to boot?"

The Q & A session was tense. Sparks flew. Voices were raised. Emotions ran high. This was democratic debate in the highest traditions of a free society. But there was no shout down, no *ad hominem* attacks, and certainly no Middlebury-style physical assault on the speaker.

For his part, Styron stood his ground, gamely asserting that when his student-critics had spent years, as he had, pouring over slave journals, then they too could write a counterpart book and roundly criticize the white author.

In contrast to the scene at Harvard, the hostility directed at Coach Kennedy, Jack Phillips, and Charles Murray illustrate the steady erosion of our nation's commitment to first freedoms: religious freedom; freedom of speech; of the press; and of freedom of assembly. So much for human progress.

So, what to do? Here are three suggestions:

First: go get elected. Easier said than done, I know, but it can be done. Time and again throughout the book, we have seen examples of why men and women of faith need to serve on school boards and city councils. What would have happened to Bridget Mergens (Chapter 5) if the Westside School Board in suburban Omaha had included one or more members who were individuals committed to faith and freedom? The story may have been dramatically different, as individuals of faith sought to make a difference in their home community.

Second: vote your faith. Take a page from my friend Sealy Yates. Appalled that in the 2012 presidential election, an estimated 25 million evangelical voters failed to show up at the polls, Sealy was led to found My Faith Votes, a thriving nonprofit organization which doesn't endorse particular candidates but, instead, simply urges individuals of faith to do their civic duty. These "values voters" shouldn't be boycotting the polls, especially in our age of growing hostility to men and women of faith. They should vote, mindful of their faith journey. If Portland Bible burners are voting, so should men and women of faith.

Third: become a genuine friend of freedom. Not in name only. That act of friendship can happen in at least two ways. Let's begin with self-education. Earlier in the book, I discussed the self-educated Abraham Lincoln and Robert Jackson, a future president and Supreme Court justice. Each of these brilliant, informally trained lawyers and public servants disciplined themselves through concentrated study to become not only superb attorneys, but masters of the English language. In similar fashion, each of us can become masters of the principles of freedom without setting foot in law school, or college for that matter. Studying this book and mastering the Great Principles of religious liberty represents an important step in becoming a freedom warrior.

The other practical and increasingly important way is to provide financial support to the wonderful nonprofit organizations dedicated to fighting for religious liberty and freedom of conscience. As I write these words, I'm sporting an Alliance Defending Freedom polo shirt. The name fits, just like my polo shirt. A short while ago, I was speaking on the phone with Kelly Shackelford, a dear friend and founder of First Liberty (Coach Kennedy's *pro bono* law firm). First Liberty's lawyers, like Alliance Defending Freedom's, are on the barricades, fighting with skill and tenacity, yet ever winsome and conciliatory. Championing the Great Principles in the courtrooms of America, they win the lion's share of their cases. Year after year, First Liberty wins over 90 percent of their cases.

These organizations, and others such as the Christian Legal Society (on whose board I serve), the Becket Fund, the Thomas More Society and the Robertson Center for Constitutional Law at Regent University, take on the forces of secularist hostility in the courtroom. It bears repeating: these noble organizations' records of success are enviable, racking up victory after important victory through vigorous defense of the Great Principles we've discussed throughout this book.

Finally, a word to my fellow freedom fighters. Let's be wise as serpents, harmless as doves. That means making wise and prudent choices, as in life, in the causes we choose to advance and the cases we take on. It was my privilege and honor to argue on behalf of Bridget Mergens in her quest to start a Bible-Study Club on her high school campus.

We were championing the core idea of equality (or equal treatment) against the forces of anti-religious discrimination. Our basic position was simple: what's fair? If the Chess Club or French Club could organize and meet on the school campus, so too could a Bible-Study club. That's a straightforward application of a Great Principle. Plus, we had a strong factual record to rely on. The litigation "homework" had been done to pave the way for eventual victory.

But we can push the litigation envelope too far. Zealous for vindicating Great Principles, we can lose sight of looming dangers, perhaps a missing link in the record or a factual stipulation that might prove fatal. For now, let's tackle "the harm principle." At bottom, this idea in its current iteration is an empty suit, inimical to the fundamental values of a free society. Let's be Churchillian. We should never give in.

As friends of American liberty, let's pledge to fight boldly and bravely for the principles of freedom enshrined in America's inspired Constitution, perfected through the shedding of blood and ratification of the post-Civil War amendments. In the spirit of Abraham Lincoln, let's push for a "new birth of freedom."

In this era of open hostility to communities of faith, let's "keep calm and carry on," with winsomeness and "charity for all," fighting the good fight and championing the Great Principles of American liberty.

AFTERWORD

In an instant, the future of religious liberty changed. The unexpected news stunned the nation, already in the throes of a bitterly contested presidential election. Justice Ruth Bader Ginsburg, a liberal icon, had passed from this life. I had known the justice well, having served with her on the DC Circuit. On the night of her passing, an invitation appeared in my inbox from the *Wall Street Journal*. I was honored to be asked to pay fond tribute to her in what turned out to be a from-the-heart OpEd piece that appeared in the *Journal* the next day.[1] The Court had lost a pioneering justice passionately devoted to the ideals of equality for all persons.

Her dying wish: that the next president, not the incumbent, would appoint her successor.

It was not to be. President Trump moved decisively to announce a list of forty potential nominees. He would move forward with a nomination, notwithstanding the vehement objections—and dire threats of court-packing—interposed by Senate Democrats. And move forward he did, with his nomination of a great friend of liberty, Judge Amy Coney Barrett of the Seventh Circuit Court of Appeals.

Her credentials were inarguably impressive. First in her class at the University of Notre Dame, law clerk to Judge Laurence Silberman of my former court, the DC Circuit, and then for Justice Antonin Scalia, she has amassed an impressive record as a teacher and scholar at her alma mater. But the key was her starkly different approach to judicial philosophy. She was of the Scalia School of constitutional interpretation, not that of Ruth Bader Ginsburg.

Bold predictions of how a newly ensconced justice will vote over the course of her career are perilous at best. Recall Justice David Souter, appointed by President George H.W. Bush, who proved to be deeply hostile to claims of religious liberty. He adhered steadfastly to the separationist ideology that dominated the High Court's thinking during the Warren Court era (discussed in Chapter 4). Ditto for Justice Harry Blackmun, appointed by President Nixon. Over the years, he transformed himself from a traditional conservative into a reliable vote in favor of rigid separationism. The same could be said of Justice John Paul Stevens, appointed by President Ford. For example, appallingly, Justice Stevens even voted against Bridget Mergens's right, both under the Constitution and federal law, to start a Bible study club at her public high school (as we saw in Chapter 5).

But Justice Barrett's life and career point to a more solidly built foundation in the nature and role of America's Constitution, and of the role of justices in interpreting our foundational document. Surprisingly, some justices ascend to the Court without a well-developed, mature constitutional philosophy. They think it through on the job, wrestling with thorny issues as they present themselves over the years.

No longer. Indicative of the polarization of twenty-first century America, judicial nominees have had these fundamental questions of judicial philosophy and worldview constantly thrust upon them. All the more so when, like Justice Barrett, the jurist has spent her career in teaching and writing about constitutional law, and then participating for several years in the judicial process.

As reflected by her magnificent performance in her confirmation hearings in late September 2020, the Court's newest justice unapologetically knows who she is and where she stands. With her seven children and loving spouse in attendance, even her detractors had to acknowledge what quickly became evident to the entire nation— President Trump had brought to the threshold of the nation's highest court an appointee of extraordinary ability and promise.

Then came the 2020 presidential election—only seven days after Justice Barrett took the judicial oath and moved her chambers from Chicago to the nation's capital. To the pundits' surprise, President

Trump won state after state, amassing over 70 million votes, and putting a lie to the pollsters' smug prediction of a "Blue wave" sweeping across America.

But the presidential incumbent's record-shattering performance on Election Day still fell short. His aging, gaffe-prone opponent—the 47-year career politician and Obama vice president, Joe Biden—rode a different wave, that of an epic number of mail-in ballots, especially flowing from America's large cities. Numerous legal challenges erupted, especially in five hotly-contested states, but the effort largely foundered.

So, what to expect in a Biden presidency? Unfortunately, the prognosis has to be unfavorable; indeed, to quote the late Justice Blackmun in a different context, "a chill wind" is blowing across the country. A stalwart defender of religious liberty for virtually his entire career, Joe Biden dramatically changed his tune during the course of the 2020 campaign. For starters, even though he is a practicing Catholic, Biden vigorously attacked the Little Sisters of the Poor for their conscience-based objection to providing the venerable order's employees with contraception services.

This aggressive about-face foreshadows a broader concern; the new administration has promised to roll back "broad religious exemptions to existing non-discrimination laws and policies across federal agencies." Leading the charge, Biden has championed the proposed Equality Act, which would significantly erode the important pro-liberty triumph embodied in the Religious Freedom Restoration Act of 1993 (which then Senator Biden had enthusiastically supported).

President Biden has reinvented himself, and now looms as a potentially dangerous enemy of religious liberty. And freedom-loving patriots need to keep a close eye on the all-important presidential appointments—some 4,000 in number—as the months-long process of forming a government unfolds. Query: What will be their worldview? It's not hard to guess.

Notwithstanding the ever-growing menace of hostile secularism, seemingly embraced in his latter years by the nation's new 46th president, with Justice Amy Coney Barrett's ascension to the High Court bench, the future of religious liberty in America—as protected in our

constitutional republic by the Supreme Court of the United States—
now seems ever more secure.

Let freedom ring!

ACKNOWLEDGMENTS

To my wonderful first-line editors—my multitalented wife, Alice, and my Baylor-trained research assistants, Jake Adams, Trevor Hoogendoorn, and Zara Kintz, whose individual and collaborative exploratory work added invaluably to the presentation; Justine Buchanan, my superb editor at Encounter Books whose brilliance was matched by her diplomatic manner of guiding the author with firmness and charm. Amanda DeMatto and Mary Spencer at Encounter immediately proved themselves to be superb guides through the labyrinthine production process.

Present at the creation was Roger Kimball, whose creativity and intellectual leadership I have long admired. We share a deep moral commitment to what T.S. Eliot astutely called "the permanent things" in our highly relativistic world. Roger and his able marketing director, Sam Schneider, believed in the book from the beginning, for which I am enduringly grateful. But before Roger came Sealy Yates, my dear friend and agent, who urged a skeptical publishing world to embrace our project. Thanks to Sealy, I came into the orbit of Seth Haines, a superb lawyer-author who helped at the earliest stages of conceptualizing the project and remained throughout a faithful editor and thoughtful critic.

NOTES

INTRODUCTION. A PRELIMINARY WORD

1 Even in aftermath of violent protests across the country in the early summer of 2020, only one "autonomous zone" was created. That zone was located in Seattle, WA.

CHAPTER 1. HANDS OFF, CAESAR!

1 Kansas Exec. Order No. 20-18 (April 7, 2020).
2 Treisman, Rachel, "West: Coronavirus Related Restrictions by State," NPR, August 13, 2020, https://www.npr.org/2020/05/01/847416108/ west-coronavirus-related-restrictions-by -state.
3 Parke, Caleb, "Florida pastor's legal team responds to 'entirely inappropriate' arrest," Fox News, March 31, 2020, https://www. foxnews.com/us/coronavirus-arrest-florida-pastor-church-update-tampa.
4 *Hosanna-Tabor Evangelical Lutheran Church and School v. EEOC*, 565 U.S. 171 (2012).
5 Id. at 13 (slip opinion).
6 Id. at 14 (slip opinion).
7 Id. at 3 (Alito, J., concurring).

CHAPTER 2. FAITH OF OUR FATHERS

1 Even the scourge of COVID-19 failed to bind the nation together, save for honoring our new heroes, the nation's health care workers and first responders.
2 First Liberty Institute, a leading national religious liberty law firm who represented The American Legion, argued that *Lemon* was incorrect, unhelpful, and needed to be set aside.
3 We will see that later in this chapter in connection with the practice of legislative prayer and the long-standing tradition of paid chaplaincies

in Congress and legislative halls across the country. Those are now safe from constitutional attack, as the Supreme Court has reaffirmed its support of religious freedom in these highly visible, highly historical, highly contextual practices.

4 588 U.S.____, at 19 (2019).
5 Id.

CHAPTER 3. FREE TO BELIEVE

1 Soloveichik, Meir, "What the Bible Taught Lincoln About America," *Wall Street Journal,* Feburary 15, 2020, https://www.wsj.com/articles /what-the-bible-taught-lincoln-about-america-11581742861.
2 Psalm 90: 10 (KJV).
3 *West Virginia State Board of Education v. Barnette,* 319 U.S. at 625 (1943).
4 Id. at 626.
5 Id. at 629.
6 Id. at 629, n. 4.
7 Id.
8 Id. at 641.
9 Id. at 642.
10 *Wisconsin v. Yoder,* 406 U.S. 205, 210.
11 Id. at 216.
12 Id. at 218, n. 10.
13 Id. at 244-245.
14 Id. at 215.

CHAPTER 4. CONSTITUTIONAL COMBAT ZONE: THE BATTLE OVER SCHOOL PRAYER

1 *Engel v. Vitale,* 370 U.S. 421, 425 (1962).
2 Id.
3 Id. at 425-26.
4 Id.
5 *School District of Abington Township v. Schempp,* 374 U.S. 203, 206 (1963).
6 In some States, including Maryland, the recitation of the Lord's Prayer was set out as an officially approved alternative to Bible reading.
7 *School District of Abington Township v. Schempp,* 374 U.S. at 208.
8 Id. at 210-11.
9 Id. at 209, n.3.
10 *Engel v. Vitale,* 370 U.S. at 429.
11 *Id.* at 442.

CHAPTER 5. DISCRIMINATION IN THE SCHOOLHOUSE

1 *Westside Community Board of Education v. Mergens*, 496 U.S. 226, 252 (1990).
2 *Tinker v. Des Moines Independent Community School District*, 393 U.S. 503 (1969).
3 *Lamb's Chapel v. Center Moriches Union Free School District*, 508 U.S. 384, 389 (1993).
4 Id. at 388, n. 3.
5 Id. at 394.

CHAPTER 6. FRIENDS IN HIGH PLACES:
THE OVAL OFFICE AND CAPITOL HILL

1 *Employment Division v. Smith*, 494 U.S. 872,877 (1990).
2 *Torcaso v. Watkins*, 367 U.S. 488 (1961).
3 *Employment Division v. Smith*, 494 U.S. at 877-78.
4 Id. at 908.
5 *City of Boerne v. Flores*, 521 U.S. 507 (1997).
6 *Cutter v. Wilkinson*, 544 U.S. 709 (2005).
7 *Brown v. Allen*, 344 U.S. 443, 540 (1953).
8 *Cutter v. Wilkinson*, 544 U.S. __ at 1 (slip opinion) (syllabus).
9 Id. at 9 (slip opinion).
10 Id. at 10 (slip opinion).
11 Office of International Religious Freedom. U.S. Department of State, https://www.state.gov/bureaus-offices/under-secretary-for-civilian-security-democracy-and-human-rights/office-of-international-religious-freedom/.

CHAPTER 7. VOUCHERS ON TRIAL

1 As an aside, losers in federal Courts of Appeals and state supreme courts can seek High Court review by filing a "petition for certiorari." The Court receives literally thousands of such petitions each year, and routinely denies the overwhelming majority; hence, the term "denied cert."
2 *Mueller v. Allen*, 463 U.S. 388 (1983).
3 *Witters v. Washington Dept. of Services for the Blind*, 474 U.S. 481 (1986).
4 *Zobrest v. Catalina Foothills School District*, 509 U.S. 1 (1993).
5 *Zelman v. Simmons-Harris*, 536 U.S. 639, 676 (2002).
6 Id.
7 Id.
8 Id. at 663.

CHAPTER 8. CAN GOVERNMENT PROVIDE FINANCIAL AID TO RELIGIOUS INSTITUTIONS?

1 *NAACP v. Alabama* 357 U.S. 449 (1958).
2 *Everson v. Board of Education* 330 U.S. 1 (1947).
3 Id. at 18.
4 Id. at 16.
5 Id. at 17.
6 Id.
7 Id.
8 Id. at 17-18.
9 Id. at 18.
10 Id.
11 Id.
12 Id. at 19.
13 Id.
14 Id. at 614.
15 Id.
16 Id.
17 Id. at 24.
18 *Board of Education v. Allen* 392 U.S. 236 (1968).
19 Id. at 243.
20 Id. at 243-44.
21 Id. at 244.
22 Id. at 245.
23 Id.
24 Id.
25 Id. at 252.
26 Id.
27 Id. at 258.
28 *Agostini v. Felton*, 521 U.S. 203, 210 (1997).
29 Id.
30 *Aguilar v Felton*, 473 U.S. 402 (1985).
31 *Agostini v. Felton*, 521 U.S. 213.
32 Id. at 225.
33 Id. at 228.

CHAPTER 9. *LEMON*'S BITTER MEDICINE

1 "Remarks by President Trump at the White House National Day of Prayer Service," White House, May 7, 2020, https://www.whitehouse.gov/briefings-statements/remarks-president-trump-white-house-national-day-prayer-service/.
2 Id.

3 403 U.S. 602 (1971).
4 *Lamb's Chapel v. Center Moriches Union Free School District*, 508 U.S. 384, 398 (1993).
5 *American Legion v. American Humanist Association*, 588 U.S. __, 13 (2019) (Alito, J., concurring) (slip opinion).
6 Id.
7 Id. at 1, 3 (Kavanaugh, J., concurring) (slip opinion).
8 Id. at 6,7 (Thomas, J., concurring) (slip opinion).
9 Id. at 7, 9 (Gorsuch, J., concurring) (slip opinion).
10 Id. at 1 (Kagan, J., concurring) (slip opinion).
11 *Lemon v. Kurtzman*, 403 U.S. at 609.
12 Id. at 610.
13 Id. at 612.
14 Id. at 614.
15 Id. at 612.
16 Id.
17 397 U.S. 664 (1970).
18 *Lemon*, 403 U.S. at 613.
19 Id. at 621.
20 Id. at 619.
21 Id.
22 Id.
23 Id. at 623.

CHAPTER 10. BEATING SWORDS INTO PLOWSHARES: THE ACCOMMODATION PRINCIPLE

1 343 U.S. 306 (1962).
2 Id. at 315.
3 Id at 313.
4 Id. at 312.
5 Id.
6 Id. at 315.
7 Id. at 319.
8 Id.
9 Id. at 324.
10 Id. at 324-25.
11 *United States v. Seeger*, 380 U.S. 163 (1965).
12 *Gillette v. United States*, 401 U.S. 437 (1971).
13 Id. at 447.
14 397 U.S. 664 (1970).
15 Id. at 668.
16 Id.

17 Id. at 669.

18 Id. at 669-70.

19 Id. at 672.

20 Id. at 673.

CHAPTER 11. DAMN THE TORPEDOES—FULL STEAM AHEAD

1   505 U.S. 833 (1992).

2   Id. at 954.

3   Id. at 966.

4   Id. at 993.

5   Id. at 860.

6   In fact, the Court remains deeply divided on the issue of abortion
    today. *See June Medical Services v. Russo*, 591 U.S. __ (2020), wherein
    conservative Chief Justice John G. Roberts offered the decisive blow to
    a Louisiana regulation that would make obtaining an abortion in the
    Pelican State impractical if not impossible.

7   *Burnet v. Coronado Oil & Gas Co.*, 285 U.S. 393, 406-407 (1932).

8   *Gamble v. United States*, 587 U.S. __, 9 (2019) (Thomas, J., concurring)
    (slip opinion).

9   Amar, Akhil. *The Law of the Land*. New York: Basic Books, 2015.

10 *Brown v. Allen*, 344 U.S. 443, 540 (1953).

11 *Fulton v. City of Philadelphia, Pennsylvania*, No. 19-123.

CHAPTER 12. RECONCILIATION AND REDEMPTION:
THE FRUITS OF RELIGIOUS LIBERTY

1   Mandela, Nelson. *Long Walk to Freedom*. New York: Little Brown &
    Co., 1994.

2   James 2:20 (KJV).

3   Matthew 5:16; Matthew 7:20 (KJV).

4   Micah 6:8 (KJV).

5   Woodberry, Robert D., "The Missionary Roots of Liberal Democracy."
    American Political Science Review 106, no. 2 (2012): 244.

6   Keefer, Mikal, "Reach Your Community Through Respite Care,"
    ChurchLeaders, April 27, 2020, https://churchleaders.com/outreach-
    missions/374490-respite-care.html.

7   Stonestreet, John, "Becoming Instruments of Peace in Times of Hatred:
    Go and Do Likewise," *Christian Post*, June 18, 2020, https://www.
    christianpost.com/voices/becoming-instruments-of-peace-in-times-of-
    hatred-go-and-do-likewise.html.

8   Id.

9   Putnam, Robert and David Campbell. *American Grace*. New York:
    Simon & Schuster, 2012.

10 In the 2020 case, *Little Sisters of the Poor Saints Peter and Paul Home v. Pennsylvania*, the Supreme Court ruled 7-2 in favor of the religious order. The extremely complex case involved ongoing conflicts between the Affordable Care Act and RFRA over the ACA's contraceptive mandate, which exempts nonprofit religious organizations from complying with the mandate.

11 Green, David, review of *Angola Prison Seminary: The Effects of Faith-Based Ministry on Identity Transformation, Desistance, and Rehabilitation*, by Hallett et al., *Punishment & Society* 21(3), July 2019, 383.

CHAPTER 13: THE RISE OF THE CANCEL CULTURE

1 *Zorach v. Clauson*, 343 U.S. 306, 342 (1952).
2 Hodges, Chris, "A Message from Pastor Chris," *Church of the Highlands*, June 2, 2020, www.churchofthehighlands.com/update.
3 Coach Kennedy is now in his sixth year of litigation without his job as a coach. He may still have years to go before his case reaches the Supreme Court again.
4 Reilly, Katie, "Conservative Writer Charles Murray Speaks Out Against Middlebury Students Who Shut Down His Talk," *Time*, March 3, 2017, https://time.com/4690735/charles-murray-middlebury-protest/.

AFTERWORD

1 Starr, Kenneth W., "Ruth Bader Ginsburg, Equality's Gracious Champion," *Wall Street Journal*, September 19, 2020, https://www.wsj.com/articles/ruth-bader-ginsburg-equalitys-gracious-champion-11600540064.

INDEX

IMAGE CREDITS

1. *The United States Constitution.* 1787. Parchment. The National Archives and Records Administration, College Park, MD.

2. *Lincoln's Address at the Dedication of the Gettysburg National Cemetery, November 19, 1863.* 1905. Lithograph. Library of Congress, Washington, DC.

3. *Dream Speech.* August 28, 1963. Photograph. AFP / Getty Images.

4. Ravi, Joe. *Panorama of United States Supreme Court Building at Dusk.* 2011. Photograph. Wikimedia Commons.

5. *Supreme Court and Justices.* October 8, 2010. Photograph. The Collection of the Supreme Court of the United States/Tribune News Service. Getty Images.

6. Garrison, Ben. *Signs of the Times.* 2020. Comic illustration.

7. Daugherty, John. *Victory Church Drive-In Service.* 2020. Photograph.

8. Stockelements. *Empty Times Square City Street with "NY STRONG" Billboard Giving Hope During Coronavirus COVID-19 Pandemic Lockdown - Nobody Outside in Manhattan NYC."* April 25, 2020. Photograph. Shutterstock.

9. *Trump Impeachment.* January 30, 2020. Photograph. Associated Press.

10. *Warren E. Burger.* March 27, 2007. Photograph. Wikimedia Commons.

11. Perna, Algerina. *Supreme Court Cross Memorial.* May 7, 2014. Photograph. Associated Press.

12. *Ten Commandments Monument.* 1961. Photograph. Capitol Historical Artifact Collection, Austin, TX.

13. Ortiz, Max. *Amish Buggy in Road.* July 25, 2019. Photograph. *The Detroit News.*

14. *Flag Salute in Public School.* 1943. Photograph. Robert H. Jackson Center, Jamestown, NY.

15. *Front Page of the New York Times, June 18, 1963.* 1963. Photograph. The *New York Times.*

16. *Prayers.* January 1, 1948. Photograph. Hulton Archive, Getty Images.

17. Dawson, Danni. *Portrait of Sandra Day O'Connor.* 1999. Painting. Collection of the Supreme Court of the United States, Washington, DC.

18. *Westside Community Board of Education v. Mergens,* 496 U.S. 226 (1990). Photo by author.

19. Solicitor General Kenneth Starr. Photo by author.

20. Harrer, Andrew. *Republican Representative Frank Wolf Interview.* February 25, 2014.

21. *Antonin Scalia.* Photograph. Collection of the Supreme Court of the United States. Wikimedia Commons.

22. Vucci, Evan. *National Prayer Breakfast.* 2019. Photograph. Associated Press.

23. Bowmer, Rick. *SCOTUS Vouchers.* 2002. Photograph. Associated Press.

24. Gash, Morry. *School Choice.* 1998. Photograph. Associated Press.

25. Schaff-Pool, Erin. *President Trump Signs Coronavirus Stimulus Bill in The Oval Office.* March 27, 2020. Photograph. Getty Images.

26. Brandon, Alex. *Trump National Day of Prayer.* 2020. Photograph. Associated Press.

27. *Cadet Chapel,* Photograph, United States Air Force Academy, Colorado Springs, CO.

28. Harnik, Andrew. *Trump Christmas Tree.* November 30, 2017. Photograph. Associated Press.

29. *Sharonell Fulton,* May 23, 2018. Photograph. Becket Fund for Religious Liberty.

30. Barrientos, Sarah. *Exchange-Church Under Bridge.* September 17, 2017. Photograph. *Waco Tribune-Herald.* Associated Press.

31. *Coach Joe Kennedy.* Photograph. First Liberty Institute.

32. Somodevilla, Chip. *Plaintiffs and Defendant in Cakeshop Case Speak to Press at Supreme Court.* December 5, 2017. Photograph. Getty Images.

33. Taitano, Kaya. *Nicholas Sandmann and Nathan Phillips.* January 18, 2019. Photograph. Reuters.

34. *President Donald Trump Speaks Next to Judge Amy Coney Barrett at the White House in the Rose Garden.* October 26, 2020. Photograph. AFP / Getty Images.

35. Roberts, Joshua. *Sister Loraine McGuire with Little Sisters of the Poor Speaks to the Media in Washington, DC,* March 23, 2016. Photograph. Reuters.

36. Public Domain. *Ruth Bader Ginsburg.* Photograph. Collection of the Supreme Court of the United States. Wikimedia Commons. https://commons.wikimedia.org/wiki/File:Ruth_Bader_Ginsburg_2016_portrait.jpg